THE FULL
MORTY

THE FULL
MORTY
DENNIS MORTIMER

With Richard Sydenham

Foreword by Bryan Robson

First published by Pitch Publishing, 2022
Reprinted in paperback 2026
1

Pitch Publishing
9 Donnington Park, 85 Birdham Road
Chichester, West Sussex, PO20 7AJ
www.pitchpublishing.co.uk
info@pitchpublishing.co.uk

Typeset by Pitch Publishing

Cover design by Olner Design

Printed and bound in India by Replika Press Pvt. Ltd.

The authorised representative in the EEA is
Easy Access System Europe OÜ, Mustamäe tee 50, 10621 Tallinn, Estonia gpsr.requests@easproject.com

A CIP catalogue record for this book is available from the British Library

ISBN 978-1-83680-490-1

Papers used by Pitch Publishing are from well-managed forests and other responsible sources

Contents

Acknowledgements

I NEVER thought I'd write a book, but 40 years after my greatest career highlight, the time felt right to talk about how and why my career turned out the way it did. It's taken a while, but we got here in the end! There are so many people to acknowledge for this journey that I have been on. I'll try to call a few names. Apologies if I miss anyone.

I would like to thank my Dad, Joe, for taking me to Anfield as a kid to watch Liverpool play. That inspired me to become a footballer and dream of winning trophies. Thanks to my brothers David, Stephen, Jeffrey and Brian who were my soccer buddies, day and night, on the streets of Kirkby, near Liverpool. I can't forget my Mum, Mary, for keeping me and my brothers nourished and energised when money was tight.

The kids and adults who lived on my street and provided the competition to hone my technique and skills; there are too many to name them all but I'll call a few: the O'Rourkes, the Caffreys, the Carines, the Burgesses, the McGuires, the Hodders and the Crosses.

I should give thanks to my senior school, Brookfield Comprehensive, for providing the playing facilities and sports coaches who encouraged me to play football. Mr Duffy, who chose me to play for Kirkby Boys at 14 years of age, which put me in the shop window to be scouted by Alf Walton, talent scout for Coventry City. Thanks to Alf for spotting the footballer in me and taking me to Coventry to begin my successful playing career.

Many thanks go to the coaching staff at Coventry for nurturing me through the early days and months after signing apprentice forms and for making me feel at home. To the landladies who looked after me when I was living away from home as a youngster. To all the players at Coventry City, especially the pros in my early days for helping us new apprentices to settle in quickly and not think of home. I'm grateful to Pat Saward (our youth-team coach) for developing me as a player and trusting his judgement when promoting me to the manager to play in the first team.

Noel Cantwell gave me my first-team debut at 17 and for that I'll always feel indebted to him. He believed in me and thought I was ready. I never looked back. I'm grateful to Gordon Milne and Joe Mercer, who replaced Noel, as they continued to show confidence in my ability by picking me every week. My old Anfield idol Gordon gave me a platform to improve my consistency in the team, which eventually led to my transfer to Aston Villa.

A massive thank you to Villa and especially Ron Saunders, who made it clear to me on signing that this club was going places and this could be the place for me to be a winner. When Ron gave me the captaincy of the team, I realised an ambition to lead the side out and go for glory. I thank the chairman and directors on their support for Ron's plans and ideas.

Huge thanks to my team-mates who made it possible to win the First Division championship and the European Cup. I regard them as mates and thankfully still see most of the '82 boys frequently. Tony Barton deserves a thank you as he kept the dream alive by believing in and staying with the existing squad after taking over from Ron. We were all rewarded by winning the biggest club prize in Europe.

Thanks also go to the fans who cheered my name throughout my career, especially those at Coventry and Villa. Last of all thanks to my wife Jan and my two boys Richard and Jon for always being there for me through the ups and downs of being a professional footballer.

I'm also grateful to Pitch Publishing for showing faith in me by putting my story into print. A special mentions goes to Jane Camillin at Pitch. And I'd like to acknowledge the contribution of my ghost writer Richard Sydenham, for keeping me on track and advising what more we needed to say, or not!

Enjoy the book,
Dennis Mortimer

Author's Note

By Richard Sydenham

'GIVE MORTY a shout,' my Mum, Linda, used to say, as me, my brother and my Dad left our house in Harborne, Birmingham, for another home game at Villa Park.

Apparently, before my time going down to Villa began as a six-year-old in 1981, her previous request was, 'Give Andy a shout.' Dad had obviously trained her well as once Andy Gray shifted to Wolves in 1979, it was all about 'Morty'. Even my sister went down to Villa a few times with her friend before Dennis's career at Villa was done so his name is firmly entrenched in my family.

If you want to read one of those autobiographies full of nightclubbing tales, alcoholic frolics and off-field mayhem, then you might want to put this book down now. You see, this is more a story of one of the most professional footballers you could wish to meet. Dennis was possibly 20 years ahead of his time in terms of the way he conducted himself and lived his life, which is why he is almost certainly Aston Villa's most successful captain in their history, added to being a great and successful player of course. As Dennis's loyal team-mate Tony Morley said later in the book, 'His manager knew he was never going to be woken up at 2am to rescue his drunken captain from a nightclub.' That kind of scenario was never going to happen with Dennis, not only because he wasn't a boozer, just because he always led by example.

Dennis Mortimer has always had a reputation with me as being the glue that held that great Aston Villa team together. A true captain. He was seemingly a reliable, consistent and reassuring presence in the midfield. His Jesus-like hair and beard maybe helped give him more of a messiah image than he deserved but Dennis was certainly one of the most significant players for Villa throughout that golden era of the late 1970s and early 1980s.

Gary Shaw, Tony Morley and, latterly, Mark Walters were always my favourite players at that time, possibly because I kidded myself that I was going to be like them one day if I continued scoring a few in school football. I think I had a better left foot than Tony, though! But seriously, there was always an admiration for Dennis.

When he phoned me at my home in the summer of 2021 and said he was serious about penning his autobiography, sounding me out to be his ghost writer, I knew in the back of my mind that I had to say yes. I played it cool for a few weeks as I became busy with my other work commitments, but there was no way I was going to pass on the opportunity to help write the story of Aston Villa's greatest ever captain.

As a 7 year old with the European Cup I am on the right, with my brother left, Dad in the middle

It was fascinating collaborating with Dennis, and I enjoyed every moment, though not paying for the £5 cups of coffee and tea whenever we conducted interviews at The Belfry! I hope football-loving fans of all clubs, especially Coventry and Villa, enjoy the read.

'Dennis could easily have got an England cap'

Foreword by Bryan Robson

I CONSIDER some players I played with and against over the years very unlucky not to have won at least one England cap and Dennis Mortimer would certainly be one of those guys.

One of my old team-mates from West Brom, Len Cantello, was another. He was an excellent central midfielder. There have been a few over the years who do such a great job for their club but don't get selected for the national team for whatever reason and are very unlucky.

Dennis could easily have got an England cap because he was just as good as his Villa team-mate Gordon Cowans, who was another excellent player and who I had the pleasure of playing with in the England midfield a few times. Once you play with these guys you realise how good they are and I'm sure if I had been given the opportunity to play with Dennis, I would have had the same opinion of him.

Unfortunately for Dennis there were so many good English midfielders around then like Ray Wilkins, Glenn Hoddle, Terry McDermott, Trevor Brooking, myself and a few others. It was a tough team to get into then.

Dennis was a very good player with an excellent football intelligence, was a worker and could pass the ball really well. I'm sure his Aston Villa team-mates would say he was a great leader, too, so these are reasons why he was captain of the team, because he had such a great influence on the players around him.

It was always tough when Dennis was in the opposition. As a central midfield player, he would make intelligent runs into the opposition's half and find space in dangerous areas of the pitch and he took a lot of care with his passing; he rarely wasted the ball.

The West Brom–Villa local derbies (there were eight between Bryan and Dennis and 13 matches in total including Manchester United clashes) were very tough and physical games. Villa were very good at that stage, while we were building a team able to compete at the top end of the table. When Villa won the league in 1981, we finished fourth, so we weren't that far behind.

The fact Villa won the league championship and European Cup in the early 1980s showed just how good they were and even in the late 1970s they were very strong, building towards those successes. Dennis was a significant part of that period for Villa. That Villa midfield was some unit with Dennis, Gordon

(Cowans), Des Bremner and then Tony Morley on the wing. They had a strong, hard-working ethic across their midfield.

I don't remember Villa belting us (West Brom), or us belting them, they were always close, hard-fought games. Most of the matches I played against Dennis – whether for West Brom or Manchester United – would have been under Ron Atkinson and Ron was never the kind of manager to say, 'We need to stop Dennis Mortimer', or any of their other players. He was more about us expressing ourselves and getting on the ball. But Ron would certainly have been very aware of the danger Dennis posed with his passing and runs from the midfield.

One thing I can recall Ron saying about that Villa team was we had to be totally focused when it came to set plays because Andy Gray and then later Peter Withe were excellent in the air and players like Gary Shaw, Dennis and Gordon were good at picking up the loose balls and causing us problems in or around our penalty area.

For me, though, the greatest strength of that Aston Villa team was the engine room right across the midfield. They never seemed to get injured, always looked fit and so were playing all the time. It was a good time for Aston Villa – I can't speak highly enough of them. The fact Dennis was their captain speaks volumes for him and his influence on the team.

I never got to know Dennis too much as a bloke off the field, but we did cross paths a few times at awards dinners and the odd social occasion like that. The Villa and West Brom lads would always shake hands, have a chat and there was a strong, mutual respect.

Bryan Robson, *(90 caps for England)*
November 2021

Growing Up, in the Shadow of The Beatles

*'It wasn't donkey rides and dodgems for us
as kids like it might have been for many.
Anything that didn't cost any money, then
we might have had a go at it.'*

I WAS born on 5 April 1952 in Everton, to a Liverpool-supporting father called Joseph and a mother named Mary. When I tell people that my Mum and Dad were called Joseph and Mary, they think I'm having a laugh. I can assure you I'm not and I wasn't born in a manger either!

I was the second-oldest of six children; first there was David, who was a good footballer and was once offered an opportunity by Blackburn Rovers but decided against it. Instead, he later owned his own steel fabrication firm. As a 6ft 1in versatile footballer who was hard in the tackle, I would liken David to the iconic Liverpool hard-man defender Tommy Smith – and I know he would have made it in the game, but it wasn't to be for him. Then after me came Stephen, Jeffrey and Brian, and the youngest of us all, my sister Karen, who has worked as an administrator in the medical world. Steve didn't play any football after leaving school. Jeff played at Skelmersdale youth team then moved to Bootle with Dave.

Brian never played football and became a builder: whether a plasterer, bricklayer or plumber, he's a man of all trades. Like me, they're all still loyal Liverpool fans. Aston Villa and Coventry will always have a special place in my heart, but you can't change what you are and I'm a born and bred Scouser.

My Dad had quite a story to tell. He was a cook in the Merchant Navy before returning to Merseyside and then worked as a sales rep for a confectioner on Scotland Road, which is a well-known road in Liverpool. He later had an ice cream van and, if we were lucky, he would take us on his rounds occasionally and allow us a choc ice – which was always my ice cream of choice!

Dad wasn't done there, either. He was a road manager – or a roadie to use the correct music scene lingo – for an up-and-coming band in Liverpool called The Denims. He would go out and get them gigs, on top of his regular work. I remember him telling me once they would make about ten quid for a night. There were four in the group so he would give them all a quid each, pay for the petrol in the van and maybe he would have a quid left over for himself despite all his hard work, getting in at silly hours in the middle of the night. He would then have to go to work his regular job the following morning. I wish I had asked Dad why he bothered doing all that, but I suspect he was just ambitious more than a fun-seeker or a night owl.

I imagine he saw the likes of The Beatles taking off and wanted to play his part in forming the next John, Paul, George and Ringo, but it wasn't to be. Outside of London, Liverpool was the place to be in those days for young musicians or artists. Growing up, I never really went into the city centre as I was too young to taste the nightlife and I left home for a new life with Coventry City at 15 to become a professional footballer so the whole Swinging Sixties movement in Merseyside kind of passed me by.

I do wish Dad was around still so I could ask him if he ever came across the Fab Four, while he was gigging with The Denims. I'm not sure, but he might well have done in those heady days. It was certainly an exciting time to be connected to the music scene in Liverpool as The Beatles, Gerry & The Pacemakers, The Merseybeats and more started to break through in Britain and further afield in some cases.

Mum's story wasn't quite as remarkable as Dad's but nonetheless she was still a hard worker who looked after us all and would then go out to her night shift at the Birds Eye factory five nights a week. You never appreciate it as kids, but I look back now and think I don't know how Mum and Dad managed to raise us all when they worked so hard to earn a living. Even when they weren't working, though, I wouldn't say we were close. Rarely did we do anything as a family. Typically,

Mum would make a roast dinner on a Sunday and instead of all sitting round eating together like most families probably would, that never really happened. If Dad wasn't working, he would probably be tinkering with a car in our garage. Mum would send one of us out to tell him his dinner was ready and he would say, 'I'll be there in five minutes.' But an hour later he was still in the garage tinkering, and by the time he would return to the house to eat his dried-up dinner that had been placed in the oven to keep warm, the rest of us would have cleared off outside to play, so the traditional family gathering wasn't really a routine we were accustomed to. The only day trips I remember us going on as a family were to visit Grandma Annie in Oswestry, before she moved back to Liverpool, near Anfield. And even those trips felt like a real painstaking exercise because the roads were so slow then that it would take what felt like a day to get there and back, never mind the visit in between.

I guess most kids would have happy memories of visits to funfairs and beaches, but we never went anywhere like that because Dad knew it would cost him money for all his kids to go on the various rides. And he never had the money to do that, so we never saw the likes of Blackpool, Southport or New Brighton because they all had a funfair. Dad instead took us over the water, across the River Mersey, to places like Moreton and Wallasey. People might be more familiar with golf courses in that area like Hoylake and Royal Liverpool. But for us, we would be ankle-deep in mud, cockle-picking. Dad would be there with us, with our buckets because he wasn't a drinker or a smoker, so he would do things like that with us but that was about as exciting as our day trips got. It wasn't donkey rides and dodgems for us like it might have been for many. Anything that didn't cost any money, then we might have had a go at it.

I never met Grandad on my Dad's side, Joseph Nathan. But I did see more of Grandma Annie, as she lived about a mile from Anfield, which was very useful when we needed somewhere to park on matchdays! She remarried and we knew her new husband as 'Uncle Albert'. I have a more vivid recollection of my mother's Dad as he worked as a 'supervisor' – though you could say 'cleaner' to be more exact – in the WC in the town of Kirkby, the other end to where we lived. Grandad Wilkinson (called Frederick) liked a bet on the horses. It wasn't unusual for him to drop in to our house on a lunchtime so he could listen to a race or two that he no doubt had a flutter on. He would always leave half a crown for the kids when he left – whether he won or not! Grandma Wilkinson, or Alice, was quite an eccentric lady and I remember her always holding a carrier bag. The reason being she was a hoarder and would pick up bits of wood off the floor that she thought would make good firewood. I wouldn't say I was close to any of my grandparents, though. I don't recall any long, memorable chats with any of them.

We first lived in a terraced two-up two-down house in Kirkby on Rusland Road. It was a bit crowded for us six kids in a house that never had enough bedrooms. I had to share a bed with two of my brothers, Stephen and Brian. That was a sign of the times when families were much bigger. Things were very different then. Typical childhood memories were of being outside and keeping busy because there wasn't much to do inside, unlike the youngsters nowadays, who are spoiled for choice with their various electrical devices and television channels. We had a black and white television, but I never watched it apart from maybe the odd early episodes of *Doctor Who* with all the daleks. But rarely did we sit down together as a family and watch television. There was nothing in our house that kept us inside. Our life then was on the street. People had big families in those days and the streets would just be full of kids outside, playing. Mum and Dad worked so much we often took care of ourselves if their shifts clashed and even if Dad was home, he wasn't with us most of the time. If we weren't playing football at the local school playing field, we'd be playing 'follow the leader' running around and jumping over walls or similar daredevil adventures that undoubtedly would have helped me become the good athlete I was later in my football career.

We would dare each other to jump across the River Alt – long before it joined the River Mersey – and I don't ever remember falling in! We also used to go bean picking for pocket money on the farmer's fields over Ormskirk way. We'd get up ridiculously early and cycle out to the countryside and fill up these sacks full of beans and the farmer would give us a shilling a sack. So, I was used to an outdoor way of life from an early age.

I don't remember how old I was when I first kicked a ball or when I started playing the game. But what I do know is that once I did start playing football, that was it. My life was just about football. What else was there to do?

My Dad was a keen Liverpool fan and would take me to every home game. He started going a lot more once Bill Shankly led them, in 1962, back to the top flight, where they have remained ever since of course. Not all the brothers went but I always did so I guess I showed the most interest in football in those days. I wish I could tell you honestly when Dad took me to my first game and recite the score and match details, but I haven't got a clue. However, I know it would be around the early to mid-Sixties when Shankly started to make a real difference to the club and set it on the path to where it is today, as one of the most successful clubs in the world. Therefore, I'd have been around 12 when they won the league in 1964. I will certainly never forget the first team I idolised: Tommy Lawrence in goal; Gerry Byrne right-back, Ronnie Moran left-back, Tommy Smith and Ron Yeats in the centre of defence – but sometimes Phil Ferns; Gordon Milne and Willie Stevenson in midfield, then that amazing forward line of Ian Callaghan, Roger Hunt, Peter Thompson and Ian St John. They were all my heroes. I didn't ever go round, when playing on the park, saying, 'Today I'm Peter Thompson' or Gordon Milne or whoever, I idolised the whole team. Maybe that's because in those days there wasn't huge exposure of players like we see today in the media. There weren't many television interviews or any internet or mobile phone coverage of course like we see everywhere now. So, your heroes were more real because if you wanted to meet them you physically had to go and see them, and I did exactly that! They were much more accessible in those days, too.

I became a collector of photos, especially pictures of the Liverpool team, which I used to cut out of the newspapers. During school holidays I would get on my bike and ride down to the Melwood training ground. They didn't let you inside, so we had to peer over the top of this brick wall that circled the training pitches. Afterwards, the players came out and would drive down to Anfield for a shower. So, we would get on our bikes and meet them down there. By the time we reached the ground, the players would invariably be showered and began to leave. This was our moment to pounce and ask the players to sign our autograph books or, in my case, the photos that I had scissored out of the papers. The players were friendly and cooperative apart from one player who sticks in my mind as being difficult to get an autograph from, and that was Willie Stevenson. He would never sign an autograph – everybody else would but he never did. Everyone was so respectful in those days. We waited in line and would all be expected to say, 'Can I have your autograph please, Mr Hunt?' or whoever. I have noticed in more recent times how people just shove a photograph or autograph book under your nose and expect you to sign it for them. If I see rudeness or people pushing ahead of other people when they want my signature, I will tell them, 'Back off, mate.'

I had a fantastic collection of autographs and signed Liverpool players' photographs. That wasn't the only thing I collected. I also had a wonderful stash of DC comics and Marvel comics: *Spiderman, Batman, Iron Man, Daredevil, The Fantastic Four* and so on. I never liked *Superman*, though.

I was doing a paper round at the age of 12 and earning a pound a week, so I was rich! Especially with the sixpence off my grandad was well. I shouldn't have been allowed to have a paper round at that age, but I did. I bought the comics with my wages and developed a great collection.

'What happened to the collections?' I hear you all saying. Well, it's a tragic story but sadly true. When my parents moved into their final house, the one they died in that was still in Kirkby but nearer to the East Lancashire Road, my immaculate, numbered collections that had been stored in a wardrobe, never made the cut of the treasured possessions deemed important enough to be shifted to the new family home. But I only found this out very recently. I obviously relocated to the West Midlands at 15 so wasn't around as much as my brothers. I asked Stephen what happened to my autographs and comics, and he said, 'Oh we threw them away because you weren't around anymore.' I was angry with myself that over those years I never went back to claim my possessions. Why didn't I say to Mum, 'Whatever you do, don't throw my things away.' I just never thought that Mum and Dad would move. I was devastated when I found out that they were thrown out with the rubbish, especially when you think of what original Marvel comics are worth nowadays. I had them all from number one all the way through. Losing the comics was bad enough but I was more upset at the Liverpool football player autographs and photos. I had spent hours waiting around collecting them.

Anyway, back to my early Anfield experiences. I have got great memories of watching Liverpool from The Boys' Pen, which was alongside The Kop. It cost Dad half a crown to get into The Kop and then a shilling for me to get into The Boys' Pen. You could see everyone swaying in The Kop, the atmosphere was incredible. The game that stands out most vividly is the Celtic semi-final second leg in the European Cup Winners' Cup in 1966. It was just after my 14th birthday. Jock Stein's Celtic team became the revered Lisbon Lions a year later by becoming the first British team to win the European Cup, so they were a tough challenge for Shankly's Liverpool.

The first leg finished 1-0 to Celtic in front of 76,446. There were more than 54,000 for the second leg and the atmosphere that night was unbelievable. I remember the steam coming off the crowd on this cold night, such was the heat they generated. I've never seen anything like it since. It was a fog emanating from The Kop, which witnessed goals from Tommy Smith and

Geoff Strong within six second-half minutes to seal the win. I dreamt of being a Liverpool footballer as a kid and it was nights like that which strengthened that feeling. Although I probably didn't think that way when the Celtic fans started throwing bottles on the pitch to try and get the match abandoned!

Liverpool went through to the final to play Borussia Dortmund, at Hampden Park in Glasgow. It was my first proper away game if I don't count Everton. A Ron Yeats own goal in extra time gave the Germans the win but this Shankly team were far from done and went on to win many more trophies; a baton that Bob Paisley, Joe Fagan and then Kenny Dalglish took on for many a year. Those early days at Anfield had a powerful, lasting impression on me. Quite simply, I was inspired to make something of myself in football. Having been fortunate enough to watch first-hand the start of the Liverpool golden era take shape under Shankly, with league titles in 1964 and 1966 and an FA Cup win in 1965, I remember thinking when I received my first pro contract at Coventry City, 'I can't play this game and not win something.'

The Talented Kirkby Kids

'(My headmaster) went on a bit of a rant about how football would not be a good life choice and I should be careful about what decision I make and that I should be staying at school for as long as I could to take all my qualifications. Was I listening? No!'

SCHOOL WAS just about playing football for me. I only ever wanted to play football. Even in sports lessons when we had rugby or swimming, all I wanted to do was play football instead. I went to Brookfield School, which was a comprehensive at the time but is an academy now. In 2009, the Kirkby Secondary School merged with Ruffwood School to form Kirkby Sports College, on the site of the original Brookfield School. It was later converted to academy status and is now called Kirkby High School.

I was never under any pressure through my school days when playing football. It was all about fun and enjoyment. Nowadays, the boys are under the microscope from age eight or even earlier with the various football club academies that exist. They serve a good purpose in one way, providing facilities and play for the youngsters, but I don't like to hear of the pressure kids are under from such a young age. I had no pressure from my parents unlike a lot of kids today.

Something that really gave my football an edge more than school football was playing casually outside of school, against men – stronger, bigger and hairier than we were at that time. We would play on the local school playing field that was situated about 100 yards away from where we all lived. I would have been about 12 or 13 then. We had matches of various ages involved – football most of the time and cricket in the summer. If you couldn't handle that added physicality, you didn't join in. Those games could sometimes see as many as 30 people playing as word spread and kids from various streets would join in. And men would finish work and join in also. The goals seemed like they were 400 yards apart so when you think the pitch was so big and with so many people playing, you hardly got a touch of the ball. But when you did, you wanted to make sure you didn't lose it too soon and did something with it. These games could go on for hours, though we might leave at different times for our tea and come back and rejoin. These times greatly developed my game in those early days.

We also played on the car park of the local pub, The Kingfisher. If that car park was full we'd go to the nearby car park at the Transport and General Workers' Union Men's Club. But the grass pitch on the local infant school was more to my liking as it was like playing on Wembley! We would jump over the perimeter fence and play. It was even better than the bigger grass playing fields. We'd get chased off it a few times by the groundsman, but it never put us off going back; not for long anyway.

My game was developing nicely, without me even realising it because I was just playing for fun. I never belonged to any one position either. There was a freedom about playing the game at that age. I would play up front for my school, Brookfield. I was a goalscorer. But I still never felt like that was the only position I could play. I actually kept a neat record of all my school matches: who we were playing against, the score, who scored, what position I played, et cetera. But not man of the match. We didn't think like that in those days; I think that was a new phenomenon as my career progressed. Those records were immaculately kept in this book and, unfortunately, it was thrown away along with my comics and signed photos when Mum and Dad moved house. But I remember, though, I used to score a lot of goals.

The major progression for me and my football began once I was selected for the Kirkby Boys' team, which was like a district team picked from the best juniors from the local schools. They were: Brookfield School, which was on the south tip of Kirkby in Southdene; there was Ruffwood School, a Protestant school which was on the other side of Kirkby, on the north side; and then there was St Kevin's, which was a Catholic all boys' school.

I started with Kirkby Boys in my fourth year at Brookfield School, so I would have probably been 14. We had trials after being put forward by our respective schools. Fortunately, I emulated my older brother David by passing the trial and we had two trophies to play for: the Lancashire Cup and the English Schools' Trophy.

We had a seriously strong group of footballers in our Kirkby Boys team. There was myself, my future Aston Villa team-mate Kenny Swain, England and Liverpool midfielder Terry McDermott, John McLoughlin – who also went on to play for Liverpool before his career ended prematurely due to injury, and Jimmy Redfern – who went to Bolton. How many school district teams can boast almost half a dozen future pros and three European Cup winners (myself, Kenny and Terry Mac)? We were all scrawny, fit, healthy boys and there wasn't an ounce of fat on any of us. I guess we were all products of our generation when our mothers didn't want us hanging around the house and we'd all play outside instead, usually kicking a football.

Kenny was from Ruffwood, Terry was from St Kevin's and I was obviously from Brookfield so we all came together from different schools, before playing in the same team together. I played on the right wing then, Terry was in midfield, Jimmy Redfern was up front with Kenny and John McLoughlin was at the back. We had a good, technically gifted side but we lacked the physicality that some other teams had. The further we got in tournaments we were probably bullied a little.

We lost a quarter-final in the Lancashire Schools Trophy 1-0 to Seaham Boys from the North East. It was a bitterly cold day, had been raining, the pitch was heavy and for maybe the only time in my career I couldn't wait to get off the pitch. It was so cold I couldn't feel my hands and I thought I was going to get hypothermia! I still remember dashing to the toilets to run hot water over my hands, which was the worst thing I could have done because my fingers were actually burning then. I couldn't feel a thing until the numbness wore off and then I was left with this terrible burn. On another day we could have won that game and, who knows, maybe even gone on to win the final.

We had a Kirkby Boys reunion a couple of years ago and me and Kenny went along, so too did Terry Mac and his Liverpool team-mate Phil Thompson, who was a year younger than us. My younger brother Steve played with Thommo at Brookfield actually. I asked Steve if he played for Kirkby Boys and he said he didn't, despite being a good technical player. It turns out he went for the trial at St Kevin's and when he got to the gates, on his own, he saw all these St Kevin's boys in their uniform and got a bit intimidated and turned back. To be fair to our Steven, it wasn't unusual then to see after-school scuffles between the local schools so I can understand why he did what he did. But it was a shame as he would have got in and played. My other younger brothers Jeff and Brian did play for Kirkby Boys though, so the family was well represented.

Word began to spread about a few of us through our performances for Kirkby Boys. A scout from Bury went to see Terry Mac, and he came knocking at my house as well. But neither my Mum or Dad were in. For obvious reasons he couldn't talk to me on my own about my future, so he left.

About a week later I got a message from my school headmaster to go and see him in his office. I'd never been to see the headmaster in my life. I was very apprehensive, to put it politely, thinking I was going to get a rollicking about something – God knows what, but I was thinking the worst. I went into his office and he wasted no time in telling me that the school had received an approach from a football scout representing Coventry City and he would like to talk to me, my Mum and my Dad. He then went on a bit of a rant about how football would not be a good life choice and I should be careful about what decision I make and that I should be staying at school for as long as I could to take all my qualifications. Was I listening? No! I just kept thinking, 'A Coventry City scout … wants to see me? Wow, this is great!'

Sent to Coventry

'[In the 1970 FA Youth Cup Final]
Graeme Souness tried to put me out of the
game with a punch but, fortunately for
me, he missed. The referee saw the intent
and sent him on his way'

THE FURTHEST I'd ever been, with the exception of a one-off trip to Glasgow to watch Liverpool play, was Oswestry to see my grandmother, or over the Mersey to go cockle-picking. But here I was about to embark on a new start in Coventry. 'Where the bloody hell is Coventry?' – that's what I remember thinking. I didn't have a clue where it was because I'd hardly travelled.

The dream of playing for my beloved Liverpool wasn't yet dead but I guess the seed was sown once I was asked to trial with Coventry. It took me on a different path. But the ultimate glory was the fact I was on the road to becoming a professional footballer, which was all I ever wanted. I never headed to Coventry thinking I had made it though, far from it. I never had a contract or any promises from anyone. What I did have though was an opportunity; an opportunity to train with them over the school summer holiday and prove that I had the ability to become a footballer. I was in wonderland to just be given the chance of playing football every day of the summer holiday with a professional club.

Coventry City's chief scout, Alf Walton, who was a larger-than-life character from Bury, picked me up at my house and we drove down to Coventry along with another lad in the car, Ivan Crossley, who had signed as an apprentice by then, but I didn't know that at the time. Ivan became my best mate for the next three years – we went everywhere together. The M6 wasn't there then so God knows which route we took, but it felt like the longest journey I had ever been on in my life. It probably was.

We reached our guest house that was about three miles away from the Highfield Road ground. The house was run by two older ladies who really looked after myself and Ivan. They were like our second mothers. We never wanted for anything. They'd make us breakfast in the morning, dinner in the evening and we'd be out training all day. We would be sharing the house with your typical travelling businessmen who came and went.

We trained most days at various facilities as the training ground at Ryton-on-Dunsmore had not been acquired at that time. Sometimes we'd go to this field near Leamington that was owned by the National Farmers' Union and that would be cross-country day. Some of the boys hated that but I was good at long-distance running so didn't mind it. The first time we did cross-country I came second – ahead of trialists, apprentices, the reserves and even the first team. They were all there. The only guy who came in ahead of me was Mick Coop, who was to become a regular team-mate of mine.

Mick was the fittest guy at the club. A good overlapping right-back, tall for a full-back at 6ft. He probably became the most consistent player we had – he never seemed to give a bad performance whether in defence or going forward. As his career progressed, he loved to play golf and it seemed if he wasn't playing football, he would be on the golf course. I usually found that guys like that lived their lives a bit more professionally than those who didn't know what to do with themselves after training.

As I arrived, Jimmy Hill was manager. He had just led their promotion from the Second Division to the top tier. But he was on his way out of management by then. I didn't get to see much of Jimmy as he was always busy doing other things, whether it was media work, negotiating for players, I don't know, but he was busy for much of the time. I saw more of his assistant Alan Dicks and the youth-team manager and former Villa midfielder, Pat Saward.

I loved every day there – what youngster who wanted to become a footballer wouldn't love playing football every day? There was not a hint of homesickness. Anyway, after three weeks I was called into the secretary's office. He said, 'Your mother has been in touch; she wants to know if you're still in Coventry?' I thought, 'Oh dear!' I wrote to her and told her everything was fine but from that moment, Mum arranged to have a phone put in at home so some good came from my thoughtlessness in not calling her up to say I was fine.

After six weeks they still hadn't told me whether they were going to take me on or not and I was starting to get a bit anxious about it. I was supposed to be starting back to school on the Monday and it was now the Friday before. Therefore, I went into the office to speak to the club about where I stood. Pat was there with Alan and I explained how they hadn't told me whether I was going to become an apprentice at Coventry or whether I was being released to go back home. Alan and Pat looked at one another and then Alan said, 'Well, I'm afraid we can't offer you a contract.' I was ready to burst into tears as I considered the prospect of going back to school and my football dream being shattered. Then these two suddenly burst into laughter; they were taking the piss. This could be the cruelty of football. Here I was, a 15-year-old boy, miles away from home, no Mum, no Dad there to support me, was worried about my immediate future, and these guys were taking the piss! Eventually Pat came clean and said they would be offering me a three-year apprenticeship contract worth £6 a week, to start on the Monday. I was the last year to finish school as a 15-year-old, thank God!

The following year the school leaving age went up to 16, with a two-year apprenticeship. I couldn't help thinking to myself, though, what would have happened if I never took it upon myself to go in the office and ask them where I stood? Were they going to just keep me on trial? Anyway, I quickly got over their prank and began to enjoy the fact I now had some security that I was on my way to becoming a professional footballer. I joined the likes of Willie Carr, Jeff Lockley, Don Peachey, Trevor Gould and Graham Paddon, who were already in the youth team. Willie was already a star in the making when I joined the club and was well liked by the fans. He was the heartbeat of our midfield for a while, very industrious, tenacious, got around the pitch well and fans will always appreciate that kind of work-rate. He did have a lot of quality as well.

I also realised that my new mate Ivan was a really tenacious right-back who loved to get stuck in. He got straight into the youth team and eventually made the FA Youth Cup Final in 1968. I spent my first year just getting accustomed to being an apprentice.

At the end of my first season at Coventry, I would embark on my first overseas trip. We had a tournament to play in Amsterdam, Holland. Once we got over there, we were all informed that we had each been allocated a Dutch family to stay with for the duration of our visit. We were introduced to our 'families' and then escorted by car to their homes. That was the only time I would be given a lift as we were given directions from the house to the stadium and were expected to make our own way there and back. I was 16 and very wet behind the ears, but it was about this time that I had my eyes well and truly opened when I walked down this one street only to see women sitting in their windows with a red light exposing their 'beauty'. They were very scantily clad and I had no idea why they were there.

A group of us found ourselves wandering down one of these streets in Amsterdam later in the week. By now it had been explained to me why these women were sitting in these windows. My curiosity was piqued sufficiently to follow the lads into one of the sex shows. We ordered a drink, which was bloody expensive. We sat there, slowly drinking our beers, waiting for this show to begin. The price meant a second drink wasn't ordered and we were persuaded to leave soon after. In case you're wondering, the tournament was a success as we lost in the final, though I'm not sure that was my overriding memory of Holland!

I didn't establish myself in the youth team until my second year, 1968/69. I broke into the reserve team that season, too, as I started to feel stronger and more physically capable of playing professional men's football.

When I went to Coventry I was more of a right-winger, but they turned me into a right-midfielder and eventually I found myself in more of a central midfield position by the end of my apprenticeship. I would say I was allowed to develop naturally as I don't recall being pigeon-holed or coached into one role. Coventry had a good thing going with their youngsters and they seemed to know how best to nurture players. They were building an impressive nucleus of young players. The fact we made it to another FA Youth Cup final in 1970, my third year as an apprentice, showed how the club invested in its youth players. They were never going to be big spenders and Jimmy Hill's philosophy was to develop quality youth players, play them once they're good enough and eventually sell them on for as much profit as they could generate. By the time I played in that 1970 final against Tottenham, I was captain and had also broken into the first-team squad.

That final was a marathon. We eventually lost after not one but two replays. Both legs finished 1-0, before a 2-2 draw in the first replay, then we lost 1-0. We had quite a good team with Mick McGuire in midfield with me, the Scotsman Johnny Stevenson on the wing – he was like a young John Robertson, Alan Dugdale was at the back – he was the nephew of the Villa legend Jimmy Dugdale – and our goalkeeper was David Icke, who became a very polished television sports presenter and latterly the son of God! David was the same age as me and we joined together as 15-year-olds. He was a good goalkeeper and the times I spent with Dave never gave me the impression that he would go all extra-terrestrial on us. He didn't end up getting taken on by Coventry and found himself playing for Hereford United in his early twenties, though wasn't able to sustain that career when he was told he had arthritis in both of his knees. The next I would see of him was presenting snooker on BBC television as David Vine's understudy; then on to *Grandstand* before he disappeared.

Getting back to that final against Tottenham, they had some useful players themselves with Barry Daines in goal, future captain and legend Steve Perryman, striker Mike Flanagan, and the biggest name of them all, Graeme Souness – before he was allowed to leave for Middlesbrough and eventually Liverpool. I wouldn't say it was a claim to fame but despite his tough-tackling hardman image, Graeme only got sent off once in his English football career – and that was for a foul on me in the first replay. He tried to put me out of the game with a punch but, fortunately for me, he missed. The referee still saw the intent and sent him on his way. That should have seen us win the game with the extra man, but they rallied to 2-2 – Daines was in inspired form.

I was facing Perryman again when we had a game against the England youth team at Highfield Road. I was probably now the leading youth player in the Coventry ranks and on the cusp of the first team. We were up against a midfield of Tony Towers, Len Cantello and Perryman but still managed to win 3-1, thanks to two goals from yours truly. As I'd had a good game, the next time they picked the England youth team I was in it! We played some Euro qualifiers and, in a weird way, I wasn't too unhappy we lost to Wales and failed to progress because it meant I was able to tour America instead for four weeks with Coventry.

It was an amazing end-of-season trip and one that I went on for the next four seasons as the new soccer scene was taking shape over there. We visited St Louis, Kansas City, Dallas, Denver, Chicago, Detroit, Atlanta, Washington and Rochester. I hung out with Billy Rafferty most of the time as we weren't drinkers –

besides, you had to be 21 to drink of course and we were still teenagers then. I was getting into my music quite a bit then and I enjoyed exploring the record shops over there and adding to my vinyl collection. It was some trip for a wide-eyed young Scouser with the world at his feet. Things were now really starting to take off for me and I only have good memories of my upbringing at Coventry.

I never came across any player there who felt they were above anyone else. There were no egos and very little in the way of belittling the younger players, which could be quite common in those days. I was always made to feel comfortable and was welcomed by the senior players. I never found any player with an attitude or who was keen to show disdain towards youngsters, which nowadays might be called bullying. It was a great club for me to grow up in and learn the game. I read my old friend Terry McDermott's book and he spoke of a tough upbringing in the game at Bury, where the first-teamers were only interested in flattening him and putting him on his arse in a 'Welcome to the first team' way. I never experienced any of that.

Teenage Rookie Takes on Beckenbauer and Best

'I still have the newspaper clipping that shows Billy Bremner with his hands around my neck, like he's trying to wrestle me to the floor. I guess it was a compliment in a back-handed way'

ON 11 October 1969 I made my Coventry first-team debut against West Ham United at Highfield Road, coming on as a substitute for Maurice Setters. Ironically, the manager of West Ham that day was Ron Greenwood, a future England manager who was to deny me an England cap again and again when I was in my heyday. He clearly didn't remember my inspired performance against his team again four months later when I started at Upton Park and helped us come away with a 2-1 win, courtesy of two goals from Neil Martin, after Geoff Hurst had put the Hammers in front with an early penalty. I'm obviously joking. More of that England snub later in the book.

Some people suggested quite early on that I was the long-term successor to Ernie Machin, but I always felt that I was more like Ian Gibson. He was central to everything and a player that I always appreciated and admired. Although I only made ten appearances in that 1969/70 season, and three times as many the season after, it seemed like I was up against household names every week, but I was totally oblivious to the stardom thing. They were just opponents to me. Take that debut, the great Bobby Moore was lining up for West Ham, yet he never even registered on my radar. I was always more concerned about what I was going to do than any opponent. I was always like that. I can't remember anything about those few minutes in the first team on my debut because I was so nervous; I can't recall if I even touched the ball. I was only 17 at the time and was probably shitting my pants. Out of interest, Harry Redknapp played in that same match, but he wasn't the reality television star then, of course, that he is now!

My full first-team debut came on 7 January 1970 in the third round of the FA Cup. I don't know who wrote my scripts, but you couldn't have made it up. It was against Liverpool at Highfield Road, which was dusted in a layer of winter snow. We drew the match 1-1 and I was played out of position on the left wing, up against Chris Lawler. These were guys I was asking for an autograph four or five years earlier: Ron Yeats, Ian Callaghan, Peter Thompson, Ian St John and now here I was, crunching into tackles against them. I read the local newspaper before the match and there was a story along the lines of 'Young Scouser Mortimer could make his debut against his heroes'. I thought, 'What the hell is that all about?' It seemed too unbelievable to be true. Unfortunately, my Dad wasn't able to be there because he was working as it was a Wednesday night match. And I wasn't picked for the replay when Liverpool won 3-0.

My favourite player during my time as a footballer was Alan Hudson. I faced him in only my sixth game as a first-teamer, when we lost to his Chelsea side, but it wasn't during his time as a Chelsea player that I really admired him; it was when he went to Stoke City. I used to love watching him on *Star Soccer*, which was ITV's regionalised version of *Match of the Day*, which went out on a Sunday afternoon and focused on the Midlands teams.

Stoke was one of the sides that would get featured regularly. Alan played in a way that it looked like the ball was glued to his feet for 90 minutes. He wouldn't let the goalkeeper kick it out, he wouldn't let the centre-halves bring the ball out or kick it up to the centre-forward; he would make himself available to the goalkeeper and try to dribble his way through the midfield to create something. Every time I watched him on *Star Soccer*, I would think to myself, 'Bloody hell, he's got the ball again.' Alan became my favourite player of all time.

Another team I played against in those rookie days of mine was Don Revie's Leeds United. You can imagine the challenge I had that day as an 18-year-old up against the likes of Billy Bremner, Peter Lorimer, Norman Hunter, Johnny Giles and Jack Charlton. They beat us 2-0 at Elland Road on Halloween in 1970 and, if I needed any evidence to prove the kind of spooky match it was for me as a teenager, I still have the newspaper clipping that shows Bremner with his hands around my neck, like he's trying to wrestle me to the floor, but I guess it was a compliment in a back-handed way. It summed up Leeds at that time. They were the most professional team going around in that day because they would do whatever they had to do to win a game of football. And if that meant rugby-tackling a youngster to the floor because he's threatening to take the piss out of their team of household legends, then they would do just that. Bremner was trying to intimidate me, but those tactics were wasted on me as I never got involved in altercations, not in those days anyway. Even when the tackles were flying in, I'd just keep doing my own thing because I was never a tackler anyway, I was more of an interceptor. Maybe that's what wound Billy up. Maybe he wanted me to react and give him the fight or reaction he was looking for. They were renowned for being a very professional team and run by a meticulous manager who, by all accounts, encouraged his players to be a bit dirty at times if it meant winning a game. There was an aura about that Leeds team and that's why they were successful; they had an edge.

In my second season, the most high-profile match I played was against Bayern Munich in the Fairs Cup, which we now know as the Europa League and formerly the UEFA Cup. I didn't play in the 6-1 defeat in the first leg away but played at home when we won 2-1. I still travelled with the squad to Munich, though. It was a very disappointing day. The weather was wet and miserable, and the result was pretty much the same as far as we were concerned. Eric McManus was in goal, deputising for the injured Bill Glazer. From Eric's point of view, it was the beginning of the end for him at the club. Ernie Hunt equalised for us to make it 1-1 early in the first half but after that it was a nightmare for us and especially Eric. On a normal day he would have saved a couple of the goals that somehow crept underneath him, maybe due to the wet conditions. He got a real bad report afterwards and only played another four games for Coventry thereafter. But, in fairness, he did go on to have a long career with other clubs like Notts County and Bradford City. But this game in Munich would be one he would have wanted to forget. If Bill had been in goal, it might have been different.

Bill was a super keeper, which is amazing considering they never wore gloves in that era. The balls in training by the end of the season would have no leather left on them and they'd be like rocks. He was a real character in the dressing room as well. Even when things weren't going our way, he would often be the one who kept us going, in the battle, purely through the energy of his personality.

Bill was one of the central characters at Coventry who enjoyed a bevvy. Most of them did, but it was the era of the drinking culture in football. I came from a background where there was no drinking culture. My Dad didn't drink, so I never drank. My Dad was a huge influence on me in that sense as we never even had alcohol in the house; we never saw it. None of my brothers were drinkers either. It would have been easy for Dad to have been attracted to that scene while driving the band around in Liverpool, but he never did. So going to a football club as a youngster, especially for away matches, I started to see what football was like at the highest level behind the scenes.

There was a serious drinking culture at Coventry, like most clubs I'm told. I just stayed away from it and didn't want to get involved. Bill certainly wasn't alone as one of the boozers. Ernie Hunt, Neil Martin, Colin Stein, Willie Carr and a few others all liked a pint. Typically, on the coach coming back from an away game the boys would get stuck into the beers and still go out once we were back. I empathise with them in a way though as I always found it very difficult to sleep after a match, especially a night game. I wish I could just put my head on a pillow and sleep, but the adrenaline would still be pumping many hours after a game. I tried a few drinks at times hoping it would help me to sleep but it never did; it just kept me awake. It wasn't for me. The funny thing being a non-drinker was that you could enjoy the days in training when your mates were struggling after a good session on the lash. I remember Colin Stein at Coventry collapsing when we were doing running one Monday morning, which tended to be the day when Gordon Milne would run the legs off us to ensure all the piss was out of all the lads from the weekend. We kept running while he was on the deck, and after about 30 seconds, he just got up and joined in again as if he just needed that little lie-down. There were players that could drink heavily but their natural fitness got them through. Terry Mac was definitely like that and Gordon Cowans was another, which we will touch on more when we discuss my Villa days. Both were slight in build, but they somehow drank without it having much of an effect the next day.

I enjoyed the experience of playing in the home game against Bayern Munich. The tie had been effectively lost before we even started after that hammering in Germany. The manager knew we couldn't make it through but in those circumstances he wanted to see some pride for the shirt and in that sense, we gave him just that. It was like playing half of the West Germany team. I never thought too much about it at the time but now it's nice to look back and reflect that I played against the likes of the great Gerd Muller, Sepp Maier and especially Franz Beckenbauer, who was so majestic and skilful at sweeper. In those days there were no live games on the television so we had to make do with what we could get so Beckenbauer's reputation was almost mythical because the most we would have seen of him was during World Cups. He was so quick over the ground; he looked so comfortable that he never even seemed to be running fast because he saw situations before most other players, so he didn't look like he was rushing.

I was getting more of a run in the team by that stage and less than a fortnight after the great win over Bayern I was preparing for my first game at Anfield, which we drew 0-0. Throughout my career it was always my favourite game on the calendar, for obvious reasons. I never got nervous about those games, but they felt different to other matches, though. Probably just because of my emotional attachment coming from Liverpool and having family at the game watching me. It wasn't like I felt nervous or any more pressure. The thought of beating those guys just felt exciting. I guess it was the ultimate challenge for me and even us as a team. It was a feeling we were able to experience later that season when I enjoyed my first win over Liverpool, a 1-0 win at Highfield Road.

Even years after I'd retired, I still had that buzz of excitement for Liverpool as a club. I was at the NEC in Birmingham for an autograph convention along with my old Villa team-mates. On the same day, a group of the 1960s and 1970s Liverpool players were appearing there as well. Forget everything I achieved myself, I just felt very excited to be around those players and couldn't help wandering over to the Liverpool veteran and right-winger Ian Callaghan. I shook his hand and said thanks for everything he did for the club. I told him how much I used to love watching him play. He was probably slightly embarrassed because the praise was coming from a fellow pro but nonetheless he seemed to appreciate my compliment. Interestingly, Bill Shankly let Geoff Strong and Ian St John join Coventry just as

I was making my way in the first team, but it never felt strange playing in the same team as them because once you forget about the back story that I used to request their autographs as a kid, you realise they're just normal blokes and fellow team-mates. I was still hoping then I would have my time as a Liverpool player one day; more so when my last manager at Coventry City, Gordon Milne, who had been a Liverpool and England icon himself, told me that he expected Liverpool to come in and buy me. I knew, though, that once Terry Mac went there from Newcastle United it was unlikely they would sign me because I was a very similar player to Terry. That's the way it panned out.

I ended up playing 30 matches for the first team in that 1970/71 season as we consolidated a mid-table finish. We were never able to finish as high again as in my debut season when we came sixth. Generally, we struggled for consistency and were usually battling to stay in the division having lost too many games that we should have won. But while I was still a rookie, I had to worry about my own game more than anything to make sure I didn't lose my spot. Noel Cantwell must have been happy with me as I felt like one of the regulars by the end of that 1970/71 season. But if I was getting ahead of myself, I was given the odd reminder by one of the greats, George Best, what it took to excel in this game. We won 2-1 at the latter end of that season against a Manchester United side including Best, Bobby Charlton, Nobby Stiles and Alex Stepney, but Besty's quality shone and was clear for all to see. I was able to watch most of the match from the bench before coming on for Brian Alderson, but I saw enough of him through our next few matches against United to know just what he was all about.

Besty was the kind of player where you just never knew where he was going to pop up because he never kept to his allocated position. If the manager wanted him to play left wing and he wasn't getting the ball, he'd just drift into the middle and do his own thing until he was able to affect the game. You could say he lacked discipline in that sense, but I don't think there would be too many managers who would have minded as he was like a magician with a football at his feet. He was clever because instead of waiting out wide where the full-back could easily mark him, he would walk around and find space and just ghost into little holes that were no-man's-land as far as a defensive position was concerned. He could look lazy sometimes but when he came alive, it was trouble as he could be unstoppable. He'd pick the ball up almost unnoticed. It was a great skill. Our left-back Chris Cattlin would get so frustrated trying to follow George around that he spent most games just wanting to kick him into the stand.

Chris was a totally different kind of player to his fellow full-back Mick Coop. Chris was always on the edge of losing his temper and liked nothing better, especially if he was facing a big-name player. If he was playing against someone like George Best he would follow him all over the park out of a commitment to keep him out the game. That wasn't always best for the team as he could find himself out of position. But he was a tenacious footballer who loved to defend. He took liberties at times with his challenges and if he was playing in the modern day, he wouldn't have stayed on the field very long. Fortunately for him, there was no play-acting in those days and players generally got up after a tackle. If they stayed down, you knew he had done some damage. It's unbelievable he only got sent off twice in his career. He was so competitive he would go round the dressing room shouting at his team-mates in their face to get them motivated for the match. He really loved playing for Coventry, I must say.

Chris was always in the zone and psyched up for George Best. He was like an assassin as he was determined that his afternoon was not going to be about Best taking the piss out of him all game. Like I have said before, generally I never went into games worrying about players on the opposition team. But players like Besty, or even Lionel Messi nowadays, you cannot help but think, 'Where's Besty?' because you know they will hurt you if you switch off for a moment.

England Glances at
Misfiring Sky Blues

*'Tommy Hutchison was simply brilliant.
When he joined from Blackpool, I felt for
the first time that the club had signed a
real top player at the right age as opposed
to a legend at the end of his career'*

IN 1969/70, we surprised everybody by finishing sixth and, subsequently, qualified for Europe. But for most of my time at the club, we were inconsistent. We even faltered with a 2-0 defeat at Wolves in an FA Cup quarter-final in 1973, which was the furthest I ever went in that competition. We always struggled to score goals, especially after Neil Martin left us. Noel Cantwell kept changing his forwards and that pattern seemed to be consistent throughout my time at Coventry. Bobby Graham and Ian St John came in from Liverpool, while at different times there was also Neil, Ernie Hunt, Billy Rafferty, John O'Rourke, latterly Mick Ferguson and David Cross. It was the one position that often gave us a headache. When we came sixth many thought we had turned a corner, but it was sadly just a freakishly good season, a bit of a one-off. So many of the match reports in the local paper were of a repetitive theme – couldn't score goals.

It's a shame we couldn't hang on to Neil and Ernie for longer as they were both quality players who did a great job for Coventry. I guess you'd call them club legends. Ernie was still only 30 when he left us for Bristol City. He lived on the edge and was always the life and soul of the party. He drove an E-type Jaguar, was charismatic and just loved entertaining and loved to be entertained, a total joker.

When you looked at Ernie you could sense that he was a fool, which I mean in a nice way. A squat-looking guy with a smiley face who always wanted to see the humour in situations. When he drank too much, he liked to train the next day wearing a bin-liner under his kit and sweat out the beer. He was already the kind of guy who was often on the edge of being overweight. We would be weighed every week and if ever you weighed more than the week before there would be a fine. But aside from all that, what a player he was. He was tricky with the ball, difficult to get the ball off, sharp in short bursts and had a great right foot to the point where he barely used his left. He'd rather use the outside of his right.

Ernie was a good team-mate because he could hold the ball up and bring others into play. But my overriding memory of him was his endearing character. He was funny, would make you laugh but wasn't interested in being cruel to others, he would more likely take the mick out of himself. I didn't play in the match when Ernie scored that famous free kick that Willie Carr flicked up for him, I was sitting in the stands, but it emphasised his majestic quality as he was a good volleyer of the ball.

Neil went on to Nottingham Forest after he left us and enjoyed reasonable success. Like I said it was a shame he didn't stay with us for longer. Neil was a typical centre-forward of that generation – good in the air, a clever footballer on the ground, very brave, aggressive and a good leader of the line. We never replaced him in my time. He combined well with John O'Rourke, who was more stylish and less direct. He wasn't as aggressive as Neil but was more creative and liked to score the more spectacular goals. If John had Neil Martin's aggression, he would have been a fantastic player because centre-halves were uncompromising in those days and you had to roll your sleeves up, but that wasn't really John's game. If a defender wanted to fight you, you needed to fight as a centre-forward and hold your ground. If you weren't made that way sometimes you could lose out in the physical battle.

Another position we struggled with was the heart of defence. We couldn't get the right men in there, or at least find the right combination. Over the years we had Maurice Setters, Dave Clements, Roy Barry, Jeff Strong and Jeff Blockley – who was keen to move on to a bigger club and he did get his move, to Arsenal.

Then there was Larry Lloyd. It was a club record for Coventry when Larry came in and he did well for us but only stayed a couple of seasons before he moved to Forest. I think the supporters were accustomed to seeing their better players move on eventually. Like the time when I went to Villa, Willie to Wolves and Mick McGuire to Norwich all pretty much in the space of six months. That was a really good midfield, but it was the Coventry model to sell players for a profit. Mick was a bit like Gordon Cowans in that he didn't run all over the field like me or Willie Carr, but he was happy to sit in front of the defence, make tackles and spray the ball around.

Thankfully for the Coventry fans, one player who did stick around for a long time, pretty much ten years, was Tommy Hutchison, who was simply brilliant. When he joined from Blackpool, I felt for the first time that the club had signed a real top player at the right age, as opposed to a legend at the end of his career. When you gave Hutch the ball, he would keep it for what felt like ten minutes. He had the ability to keep hold of the ball, give the rest of us a breather, and he could just drift past players and keep control of the ball. I guess it would be like how Jack Grealish played at Villa in more recent years. He had great ability and understandably became a favourite with the fans. He is revered even to this day around Coventry and brought a genuine entertainment factor.

Maybe a lot of managers would have pulled their hair out to see so many of their top players sold to fund new signings and ground improvements, but Gordon Milne seemed to get the Coventry City vision. He kept the club in the First Division (now the Premier League of course) in each of his nine seasons as manager at Highfield Road, which was an incredible achievement given the limited resources he had. I enjoyed playing under his management. It's ironic that Gordon was my manager as he was someone I used to queue up in front of to get his autograph a few years earlier. Similarly, I played with Ian St John, another hero of mine when I was younger, but I don't remember having a cup of tea with any of them and talking about the glory days at Anfield or telling them how I used to idolise them when I was a kid. Maybe I did, but I don't remember it.

Gordon had a great career with Liverpool and England and although he was new to management in those early days at Coventry, I always felt like he was striving to find a settled team, like what he had been accustomed to under Bill Shankly. He wanted to give continuity to the players and that was probably the best thing he did for me. Before Gordon came in, both myself and the team weren't consistent and he began to pick more of a settled team with players in settled positions. By that time, I was a number four central midfielder after having been a number seven out wide on the right. So clearly Gordon saw something in me that he wanted to see more of in the middle of the park. The fact that I eventually caught the attention of England manager Don Revie would partly be down to the influence of Gordon and the confidence he instilled in me. Gordon was a quiet operator and wasn't a shouter, that was more for his assistant Tommy Casey, who liked to run us hard when Gordon didn't take training. He could be quite an intimidating character. Joe Mercer was also around then but he never came out to training and was more in the background. Joe had got the T-shirt after being successful as a manager with Manchester City. It was a good set-up as he was a useful go-between in the middle of Gordon and the board. It allowed Gordon to focus on what he was doing on the training ground.

During my final season at Coventry in 1974/75, Revie invited 100 players to a hotel in Manchester to introduce himself to all of us. It was a clear hint I was in his thinking for the England squad. Even if I was nowhere near the team at that time, I was at least in his thinking. I also got an invite from Revie to play in his first England team for a testimonial for an FA doctor, so it was another positive sign. Unfortunately, I had to pull out as I had a match with Coventry. But it was more evidence and recognition of my progress.

My football career was progressing nicely, but something else happened to me around those mid-1970s years which was significant: I found the love of my life.

I met Jan in 1973 at Rebekah's nightclub on a Saturday night in Birmingham after a Coventry match. Myself and Mick McGuire would always take ourselves off to Birmingham after games as nobody knew us over there. We knew if we went out in Coventry we would be pestered by fans, especially if we had lost that day. But we tended not to get noticed in Birmingham. I usually drove as I didn't drink. So, that's how it happened.

I had a dance with Jan, who was a Birmingham girl, and we then made plans to have a first date. That's how it worked in those days of course as there were no mobile phones to text one another on. She told me the name of this pub (The Wayfarer) to meet her in on the Stratford Road, so there I was, fighting with a map on my lap as I drove over hoping I didn't get lost and turn up late. Through good luck, I managed to find her and the romance was born.

We were married on 15 July 1975 at St Peter's Church in Hall Green, Birmingham, close to where Jan lived then. I had to miss the first day of pre-season for the ceremony as we had planned to wed during our summer holiday, but Jan's sister was away, so it meant I had to ask for permission from the club to take a day off. The best part of that was it meant we had our honeymoon in Corfu before our wedding, so in the photos we looked as brown as berries. Nowadays you see the young girls with their spray tans or fake tan rubbed all over them, but we didn't need that for our wedding as we looked like a couple of film stars by the time we had topped up our suntans.

I'm Signing for Aston Who?

'A fringe player in our squad [Keith Masefield] came to me and said, "I've been thinking … you're not very good, are you?" I was a bit stunned and said, "What do you mean?" He said, "Well, we paid a lot of money for you – and you've been rubbish!"'

WHEN DAVID Cross told me in the Coventry City dressing room at training on the morning of Monday, 22 December 1975 that Aston Villa wanted to sign me, I would be lying if I said I was excited or knew much about them. It was almost a case of, 'Aston Who?'

Don't forget, Villa had been in the lower divisions most of the time while I had played in the top flight for Coventry, so it's not as though we're talking about where they both are nowadays. Crossy didn't exactly whisper it to me either. That was the way it was in dressing rooms then; they were generally honest places. He just said, 'My ex-manager was on the phone to me about you last night, making a few enquiries.' He played under Ron Saunders at Norwich City a couple of years earlier. I never thought too much about what Crossy told me and just brushed it aside. I'd heard rumours before that Leeds United wanted to sign me and nothing happened, so I wasn't about to start reflecting too long on any speculative transfer talk now. I might even have got away lightly with the Leeds move not materialising. I'd heard from one or two people that the Leeds players at that time were quite insular and it could be a difficult place to walk into as a new guy. By all accounts it wasn't unusual to get a few nasty tackles from the likes of Johnny Giles and Billy Bremner as a kind of 'welcome to Leeds' introduction.

Crossy was a tall centre-forward and quite underrated. His work-rate was outstanding, he was a good goalscorer and with the right ammunition, was a dangerous player. As a bloke he was chatty and friendly and quite intellectual, and would hang around a lot with Mick McGuire, who stayed on at school and was another bright guy, as his latter career at the Professional Footballers' Association would show. So, what I am trying to say is he wasn't the type of guy who you would think was winding me up about this Villa talk.

Very soon I was to learn that Crossy was on to something. The Coventry secretary Eddie Plumley called me the next day and told me to get down to the ground. He informed me, rather than asked me, that I was being transferred to Aston Villa, for £175,000. It all came as a bit of a shock because I was very loyal to Coventry City at that time and thought we were going places with a talented young squad under Gordon Milne. However, as Gordon drove me to the iconic Malt Shovel pub on the A45 between Coventry and Birmingham he politely advised me that declining the move was not really an option. By 10.30am I was climbing into Saunders' Jaguar and being driven to Villa Park to sign.

We spoke in the offices in the North Stand and there were no agents around then, of course. I had no assistance whatsoever with what was about to become the most significant transfer I ever made in my football career. There was just Ron, the secretary Alan Bennett and me. They showed me the contract and I just said, 'Where do I sign?' because by now it was obvious Coventry no longer wanted me, so I knew I had to make myself a new home at Villa. I wasn't stupid, I checked the money on offer and it was exactly what I was on at Coventry – £100 a week. I wouldn't have signed for any less. Ron had presumably spoken to Gordon about what wage I was on. I also received five per cent of the transfer fee as a signing-on bonus, which was about £8,000, a lot of money in those days. Not long after I had joined Villa, I had a letter from Coventry. It was a cheque for £3,500 as a loyalty bonus. I had no idea I was due that, but it must have been in my contract. Happy days!

I understand Jimmy Hill came back to Coventry about the time I left and Jimmy was all about developing young players from the youth team and eventually selling them on for a big profit. It was ironic because Jimmy left Coventry when I arrived and came back when I was sold so I never had anything to do with him directly. I don't think my sale went down very well with the Coventry fans as Gordon was building quite a vibrant young team then, but finances always came first and that was to be the end of my time at City.

I didn't have any time to reflect on my Coventry career coming to an end. I signed on Christmas Eve and made my debut on Boxing Day! I can't say I didn't have any self-doubts then, though, despite whatever confidence I had in myself as a footballer. I thought, 'Wow, £175,000, for me? That's a lot of pressure, so I had better live up to the expectation.' Footballers shouldn't worry about transfer fees as we have no influence on them but it is only natural that you think about it and wonder if you're worth all the money.

When I started at Coventry, I had grown up with all the young players and even the senior players would have been aware of me. But at Villa I didn't know anyone, and nobody knew me, so it's only natural that everyone at Villa would be thinking, 'How good is this lad going to be?' I had to hit the ground running because a lot of money had been invested in me. Ron would have done his homework and knew what I was about, but he would have been in the minority. I didn't know about Andy Gray, Brian Little, Leighton Phillips … none of them. I was starting all over again.

My first training session was on the Wednesday, Christmas Eve, as we had to prepare for the home game against West Ham United on the Friday – the same team I had made my Coventry debut against six years earlier by a strange coincidence. I was so nervous when approaching that debut that I couldn't eat. I lost weight going into that match because I knew I was in the spotlight and had to perform. It wasn't a position I had been in before, except for maybe my early days when I was trying to impress coaches when on trial as a 15-year-old at Coventry. The main difference this time was that I had a great big transfer fee on my head to live up to. Fortunately, my confidence was high because I had been playing consistently well at Coventry that season so that stood me in good stead.

I had a good dinner on Christmas Day with Jan and her family but all through the meal I couldn't stop thinking, 'Don't eat too much because you've got your debut tomorrow!' I had a glass of champagne for the toast but that was it as far as alcohol went. Jan's family were not really that keen on football, but they were all excited for me. Jan's sister worked at ITV with Gary Newbon so no doubt she had spoken about the move to Gary and knew what it meant.

On the day of the game, I could only manage a small breakfast beforehand. It's a bit of a myth that players have a huge pre-match meal. The only time we had a pre-match meal was at away games when we would have a rump steak, no chips, just a steak. Maybe some tea and toast with jam on for after. It was soon game time.

I lined up in the middle of the park alongside Frank Carrodus, with Ian 'Chico' Hamilton to the left of us and Ray Graydon on the right, with Andy Gray and John Deehan up front. It was a classic 4-4-2 formation but over time it became a 4-3-3 or a 4-4-2 with one winger and three in central midfield. Over the next few seasons that midfield would be jiggled around a bit more until Ron found his perfect combination. There was another formation used when Brian Little came in and played in that hole behind the striker that he preferred.

Initially, I didn't see Villa as a step up. But when you consider the last attendance I'd played in front of at Highfield Road was just 14,419 for a home match against Everton, the gulf between the two clubs soon became obvious when I ran out for my debut at Villa Park in front of 51,250. The noise was deafening and there was a paranoid voice inside my head asking, 'Have they come to watch and judge me or are they just watching Aston Villa?' I was also worrying a little about whose toes I was stepping on. When a new player comes in it's inevitable that another player is going to be losing his place. Steve Hunt, Bobby McDonald and Frank Pimblett were three who probably wouldn't have appreciated my arrival. I was effectively taking their place. The truth is, though, Ron didn't fancy them. Whether it was their attitude or something else I don't know, but he wasn't having them. I met Bobby Mac in recent years, though, and he was very polite and complimentary towards me and was far from bitter that it never worked out for him at Villa. He said words to the effect that he appreciated what I did for Villa even after he had moved on. He clearly retained some affection for the club having come through the youth system. I remember Frank being a good footballer and playing in the semi-final of the League Cup the season before I arrived. He could sit in front of the back four and pass the ball around nicely, but I suspect Ron wanted more from his midfielders, like an engine to get up and down as well. There was no doubt I had trodden on toes when I landed at Villa Park.

Despite the various politics of the team manoeuvring, which I was oblivious to, I really knew I had arrived at a big club and the pressure was on. The eventual 4-1 win was what I needed to help me settle in but, more importantly, it was crucial to the club as they had only been promoted months earlier and were finding their feet in the top division. Results were inconsistent in that 1975/76 season and we would only just manage to survive by the time of the following summer. We finished in 16th, two places below Coventry, and nine points above the relegation zone. Villa had been knocked out of the UEFA Cup by Royal Antwerp a couple of months before I arrived and it was clear Ron was ruthlessly trying to find the players and the combination that he could progress this club with. Some fell away in that process and the next year would see the departures of players like goalkeeper Jim Cumbes, Bobby McDonald, club veteran Charlie

Aitken, Ray Graydon, Pat McMahon, Steve Hunt, Chico Hamilton and skipper Ian Ross.

Ron was a quietly spoken man of few words and he never said to me 'this is the role I want you to play' or 'this is what I am looking for from you'. But when he spoke you were never in any doubt about what he wanted from you or the team.

It was a sign of the times we were playing in then that my second match was the very next day after my debut, at Derby County. We lost 2-0 at the Baseball Ground, which wasn't a nice ground to go to because it was always a bad pitch. It just summed up our inconsistencies of that season that we were able to play so well one day against West Ham and then lose to Derby the next. We should remember though that Derby were the reigning league champions at the time.

My next win that season was on 19 April against, ironically, Derby County. It was a real struggle of a campaign. Villa beat Manchester United in the February while I was injured but that was our only win in four months. Still, there was no rousing speech from Ron about the dangers of relegation. In fact, I'm certain he never raised his voice in the entire time I was a player under his management. If he was ever going to do that it would have been on the training ground as opposed to the dressing room on matchdays, but even then, that wasn't his style. He had this reputation as a hardman who rattled the bones of players, but I never saw that. He was menacing in a quiet way. He had enough authority about him to not have to shout. It was probably his calm nature that stopped players from panicking during this relegation scrap.

The injury I referred to was the biggest disappointment of the season for me. I was so excited to get back to Villa Park for my second game there, three weeks after my debut, to play against Newcastle United. But just ten minutes into the game I had to be substituted when I injured my knee – again! Malcolm Macdonald caught me with a nasty, high tackle with his studs on the lower part of my leg and the weight of the tackle twisted my knee. It was the fourth consecutive season I had injured my knee ligaments and I knew what I was facing as soon as I felt the twinge. I was walking off the field totally gutted, because I knew I was facing at least two months on the sidelines, if not more. All I wanted to do was keep playing and prove myself to Aston Villa's players, supporters and, of course, the manager. I also wanted to build on the encouraging signs I had received from Don Revie to build an England career, but it all had to be put on hold.

The rehab wasn't straightforward either. I was told to report to Villa Park on Monday morning with my heavily bandaged knee as the training ground at Bodymoor Heath wasn't yet equipped with a physio room. Instead, I was met by this antiquated machinery in a dingy room, where Pat McMahon was also receiving some treatment. There was no training kit for me and I had to receive my treatment in my civvies. The physio, Fred Pedley, applied some ultrasound to the knee and said he would repeat it again in the afternoon. I had been through this injury before and I knew what I had to do to get over it. And it wasn't ultrasound in some dingy physio room at Villa Park. I needed to be doing weights, stomach exercises, as much training as possible that didn't put any aggravation on the injured knee. I had to keep a level of fitness in my body. If I had listened to Fred, I would have totally lost my fitness while recovering from this knee problem.

I went in to see Ron the next day and told him that I couldn't carry on with Fred's rehab programme otherwise I would lose all my fitness. I asked him if he would mind if I returned to Coventry City to get my injury sorted out. He had no issues with my suggestion and was a bit embarrassed and explained that he was trying to get a new physio in and was also keen to have a physio room installed at Bodymoor Heath. The Coventry physio, Norman Pilgrim, was happy to have me back and he helped return me to match fitness. It was a bit of an indictment on Villa that one of their new signings had to return to his old club to get fit, but that was how it was.

I made my first-team comeback on 6 March against Ipswich Town, so I was out for just under two months in the end. It was a huge disappointment because it upset my rhythm and I never returned to my best form for the rest of that season, even though Ron continued to pick me in the team. It didn't do much for my paranoia as I was still conscious that the fans and my team-mates were making their minds up about me.

Off the field, I was getting to know the lads ok but was never one to be taking the piss out of anyone. I probably got along with John Robson better than anyone else at first. I wasn't exactly buddy-buddy with him or anyone else. Some of the lads were more outgoing than others, which is normal for a football dressing room. I don't remember anyone being too loud. Andy (Gray) was still young and in his first season after coming down from Scotland, but he was scoring goals and was a very confident young man. John 'Budgie' Burridge was very funny and liked to take the piss out of himself rather than anyone else. The lads laughed with him rather than at him. I went round John's house once and he was wearing a three-quarter coat full of sand in the bottom because he was trying to build up his thighs as he was quite small for a goalkeeper. He had a great spring in his legs, probably because of these exercises he put himself through. I tried that coat on and it weighed an absolute ton! I've since heard Budgie say he was bullied by Ron at Villa. I can't honestly say I saw anything of that nature, but maybe it went on privately. I always felt there was a healthy atmosphere in our dressing room and never witnessed anything like that from Ron, but I don't doubt things were sometimes said behind closed doors.

It was a frustrating start for me at Aston Villa. I finished the season uncomfortable in my own skin. After that knee injury I played just one reserve game against Hereford United and I would have liked a few more to properly get my match fitness back. But I guess

Ron thought he had paid a lot of money for me and wanted me back in the first team. The upshot was that I never returned to my best form and it didn't sit well with me. I wasn't good for the team at that time and the team were losing a lot of games, so they weren't good for me either. Sometimes you can coast through games when you're getting your match fitness back in a side that's winning, but when that team is struggling, times are hard all round.

I was also down about the fact I was falling behind in the pecking order for the England midfield places after Don Revie had indicated I was in his plans. Tony Currie, Alan Hudson, Dave Thomas, Gerry Francis, Ray Wilkins, Trevor Brooking and others were all starting to receive opportunities and I had fallen behind.

If I wasn't down enough about my situation with Villa and England, my mood sank even further on an end-of-season tour to Martinique. We were all out together one night and this lad by the name of Keith Masefield, a fringe player in our squad who was a bit mouthy and anti-authoritarian, came to me and said, 'I've been thinking … you're not very good, are you?' I was a bit stunned and said, 'What do you mean?' He said, 'Well, we paid a lot of money for you – and you've been rubbish!'

I wish that was the only negative feedback I had to put up with in those early days. It wasn't. We had a player of the year award ceremony at the Grand Hotel in Birmingham. It was there that this lady supporter stared me up and down and said, 'When are you going to start playing [well]? You've been useless!' The Masefield comment came on the back of it. I couldn't have felt more shit about myself. I certainly didn't feel the need to explain that I was lacking rhythm after my injury. I knew then that pre-season and the following campaign were going to be huge for me. It was make or break time.

The Game of Our Lives – and a Cup Win!

'When you walk off the pitch having blown away the best side in the world 5-1, you can't help thinking to yourself, "Bloody hell, we're one hell of a team!"'

THE BEST thing about the 1976/77 season for me was that it meant the 1975/76 campaign had ended! It wasn't exactly an auspicious start to my Aston Villa career with the return of my knee problems and nagging doubts from team-mates and supporters as to whether Ron Saunders had signed a dud. I knew he hadn't, but it was now time to prove it.

I loved pre-season because I saw it for what it was; a way of putting some fuel in the tank for the rest of the season. Some players hated the hardship of the cross-country running and such like as it's never easy to up the ante when fitness is concerned. It's not meant to be easy. I liked it because once I got my fitness up, I always felt comfortable all season. Ron pushed us hard and it suited me and was what I needed.

We had a good pre-season tour in France. I remember going to Saint-Etienne and winning 2-1. The most telling memory I have from that trip is Keith Masefield approaching me, again. He looked at me, nodded, and said, 'I was wrong about you, you're a good player, aren't you.' He hadn't seen the real Dennis Mortimer the season before but now I had started to get somewhere near my optimum fitness he started to see what I could do. Keith was only a young lad and wasn't much of an authority in our dressing room, but he was clearly opinionated. Any player's feedback hurts when it's not complimentary, so I respected him for being big enough to change his opinion of me.

That pre-season tour was tough but they always were under Ron. He wanted to test us in Europe and he wanted us challenged by the opposition. He wasn't a big one for playing local teams and winning 10-0, which doesn't really prepare you for a tough campaign.

This season was something of a watershed for Ron and us as a team because, as I alluded to in the last chapter, he made so many personnel changes to the squad. It's well documented that Ron built three teams in his nine years as Villa manager. This was now his team number two taking shape. Our skipper Ian Ross was moved on as while he was a good defender he lacked a bit of height. Leighton Phillips was shifted from the midfield to the centre of defence alongside

Chris Nicholl – they were outstanding that season as a defensive combination. I was a big admirer of Leighton as he was a mobile defender and wasn't afraid to bring the ball out from the back. Chris was a brave warrior of a defender and would stick his head where most people wouldn't put their boot, which is why his nose was broken a few times.

Leighton going to the back opened the midfield up to change. The silky Alex Cropley joined us from Arsenal and a teenage Gordon Cowans started to feature a lot more after making his debut the previous season. Those two along with myself and Frank Carrodus generally took on the midfield positions, though the shape was occasionally altered due to injuries as we went along. I only missed one league match all season and was pleased to get through those 41 league games as it put to bed any nagging doubts about me being injury prone.

Curiously, after I made my debut against West Ham for both Coventry and Villa, the Hammers were again the opposition for the first game of my first full season at Villa. And Ron Greenwood's team didn't disappoint again as we brushed them aside 4-0, all second-half goals. I would say the way we lined up for this match was the start of the famous Ron Saunders formula that he used throughout our league championship and European Cup-winning campaigns. John Burridge was mostly in goal, though the talented Jake Findlay deputised for him at times. Jimmy Rimmer usurped both of them at the end of this campaign. John Gidman was our rampaging right-back, in the same way that Kenny Swain was in the early Eighties. John Robson and Gordon Smith shared the left-back duties like Gary Williams and Colin Gibson did four years later, while the uncompromising Chris Nicholl was a similar player to the man who replaced him at the end of this season, Ken McNaught. Leighton was a bit more cultured than Allan Evans, who was probably a better defender, but both were terrific partnerships. Myself, Frank and Alex was a similar midfield three to myself, Gordon and Des Bremner, while Ray Graydon was the lone wolf out wide in the same way that Tony Morley was later on. The goal-getting partnership of Andy Gray and Brian Little, again, was not dissimilar to that of Peter Withe and Gary Shaw, in how they linked up and one fed off the other.

We won four of our first five games and I felt we were playing some fantastic football and were all so confident in each other. The way we were playing was reflective of what we had done in the summer friendlies and was all about counter-attack. The way Ron had got us playing was electrifying at times and it was just how I liked to play. Ron was not one to dictate how we played, though. He was like a conduit and didn't preach much. He identified the players, he knew what we could do and left us to organise ourselves on the field.

I knew what Brian Little's strengths were or what Andy Gray's assets were and it was like that throughout the team. We knew Giddy was good going forward and liked to attack and put crosses in, so Frank would fill in for him. We just blended naturally and the combination in this campaign just felt right. We had a fabulous understanding of our own roles and each other's roles. We played with pace and innocence – there was no holding back and, unlike today's game, which is like watching chess, there was nowhere near as much cautiousness. The last thing on my mind was that I had to sit in the middle of the park and be the link between the defence and the midfield. I had an opportunity if I wanted to, to go forward, and I might have left the back four exposed at times, but I knew I had to get back if I did that.

We were on fire that season, reflected in the goal returns from our three strikers: Andy Gray (29 in all competitions), Brian Little (26) and John Deehan (18). Andy rightly won the Player of the Year and Young Player of the Year. He was a terrific focal point of our play, though he would be the first to admit he couldn't have scored all those goals without some pretty special football going on behind him, helping to set him up so often. But good luck to Andy as he was a fantastic finisher in those days.

Goals wasn't something I was known for, sadly. I scored my first Villa goal in a 5-1 demolition of Arsenal, which was a typical goal of mine from outside the box. The biggest criticism of myself from my career is that I didn't score enough goals. I managed 36 in all competitions and given I played over 400 games in a strong team most of the time, I should have scored many more. In fairness, though, we did have some very prolific goalscorers while I played like Andy, Brian, Dixie (Deehan), Shawsy and Withey.

The addition of Alex Cropley from Arsenal brought an extra dimension. Our midfield now had a great balance to it with Alex's wand of a left foot, along with myself, Frank and sometimes Gordon when he played. Alex was a quality player who had a lot of energy and for a small guy he had incredible tenacity in the tackle. I used to cringe when I saw him going in for a challenge. He was one of the best tacklers I saw in my career – he was fearless. Maybe that's why he broke his leg a few times. He was so committed to winning the ball that he possibly found himself over-doing it at times. I saw quite a few broken legs in my career and generally they had more to do with the challenge than an accident. Gordon Cowans was the best player I ever lined up alongside but if Alex had managed to stay fit for longer, he might also have been somewhere near Gordon's level as he was an exceptional player.

One of those early wins of the season came against Manchester City in the League Cup, who were defending the trophy they had won the season before. The 3-0 win set us on our way and it was to become a happy competition for us that season. We beat another of our manager's former teams, Norwich, in the next round and were then given a couple of fortunate draws against Third Division Wrexham, who we beat 5-1, then Millwall (2-0) in the quarters.

While we would have been expected to beat Wrexham heavily, there were quite a few results of ours that season that would have caused sections of the media, especially outside of the Midlands, and managers of other clubs, to sit up and take notice of us. We were scoring lots of goals, playing fast, vibrant, counter-attacking football and blowing teams aside at times. The 5-2 win over Ipswich was one example, when Andy Gray bagged himself a hat-trick. This was an Ipswich team with John Wark, Mick Mills and Kevin Beattie that finished above us in third that season and won the FA Cup the following campaign.

We did the same to a formidable Arsenal side the following month, picking up that 5-1 win against the likes of Alan Ball, Pat Rice, Liam Brady, Frank Stapleton, Malcolm Macdonald, Peter Storey, a young David O'Leary and a guy called Jimmy Rimmer in goal.

But the standout result from that season that is still talked about now is the 5-1 victory we had over Liverpool at Villa Park. They would go on to win the league and the European Cup, but we absolutely hammered them. It was not as though they had all their stars out injured either. They lined up: R. Clemence, P. Neal, J. Jones, P. Thompson, E. Hughes, R. Kennedy, T. McDermott, K. Keegan, D. Johnson, S. Heighway, I. Callaghan. They didn't know what hit them as we were 4-0 up just after half an hour and it was 5-1 at half-time. Our dressing room wasn't too over-excited at the break because that wasn't Ron's style. He just said, 'Keep it going, don't drop the pace.' We knew they had enough quality in their ranks to come back if we allowed for any complacency. That never happened and we battered them again in the second half but just couldn't find the net. It could easily have been seven or eight by the final whistle. It was the game of our lives.

We didn't even have our strongest team out as our skipper Chris Nicholl had a broken nose and was replaced by the rookie Charlie Young. Even our sub was another rookie, Mike Buttress, while our regular keeper 'Budgie' Burridge was missing with Jake Findlay deputising for him.

It was frustrating that despite winning a game as tough as that, as convincingly as we did to go third in the league, we still finished in sixth and six points behind Liverpool. We were better than that. But quite often the reason for these results is you can only play as well as the opposition allow you and I imagine Liverpool would not have expected that performance from us on that night after they beat us 3-0 at their place a few weeks earlier. We caught them napping and the pace of our football was frightening. They would not have experienced 45 minutes like that before this match or afterwards. I had Liverpool friends telling me that fans were late for the game trying to get into the ground and thought people were taking the mick when they were told they were 4-0 down – while they were still queuing up. It's annoying there wasn't one television camera to capture the footage.

We were an exciting team for our fans to watch and possibly even for the neutrals. We never drew a single match for the first 16 games of the season and while that indicated we could be very gung-ho and liked to go for the jugular, maybe it also cost us. I can't help thinking if we had drawn more of those matches we lost we would have won the league. That might sound funny as we were sixth but when you consider we were only six points behind the champions, I can't help wondering what might have been possible if we had drawn more of those matches we lost.

Middlesbrough, for instance, was a ground we usually struggled at. We never won there in seven consecutive seasons from 1975/76 through to 1981/82, when they were relegated as the bottom club in the division. I don't know why we struggled against them, but we always did. Ayresome Park was a place where we should have always drawn or won. Maybe it was the long journey, but they also had a few decent players like Graeme Souness early on and then David Armstrong, Craig Johnston and the keeper Jim Platt. Even our great rivals Birmingham City did the double on us that season and were the only team to beat us at home. But we lost as many as 12 games on the road, which was far too many and ultimately lost us the title, even though we were huge underdogs. As disappointing as it was, we were still only in our second season since being promoted from the second tier and we lacked that know-how and pedigree to grind out results, which was a quality we acquired more over the next few seasons.

We were a work in progress still. Exciting for sure, but still developing.

The League Cup was our biggest triumph of the season. After overcoming Millwall in the quarter-finals, we faced Queens Park Rangers in three semi-finals. First the usual double-legged affair and then a replay, which we won 3-0 at Highbury. Who knew another triple encounter lay ahead in the final!

The upcoming three-match final against Everton and those three semis against QPR really took their toll on us in terms of fatigue from the subsequent fixture pile-up. We had 15 league matches in April and May when Liverpool had ten in comparison. We had seven league games in 19 days in May when the runners-up Manchester City had only four. It cost us dearly. I have heard one or two suggest we lacked professionalism in failing to grind out draws from what were losses, but I don't agree. I don't feel we ever came off the field having given anything less than 100 per cent. We were just running on empty and injuries to key players like Giddy, Frank and Alex at different times hurt us.

Wembley was such a disappointment. The biggest problem we had in that game was the boredom. They cancelled us out and had clearly set on a game-plan of just slowing us down and they succeeded in that. I read a newspaper report somewhere that said Everton made 82 back-passes to the goalkeeper. I guess their plan worked as our game was about counter-attack and for that to work, we needed teams to attack us but Everton had very little interest in doing that. It was such an empty feeling to walk off the Wembley pitch and not have a trophy or a medal to pick up. We went to the reception later that had been arranged, even though there was nothing to celebrate, and I felt like I couldn't remember what I had been doing that day. Everton really bored the pants off us and nullified everything we had to offer. It was ultimately a compliment because teams knew how dangerous we were, which stemmed from our training when everything was done at match pace.

I have never watched the game back since and I probably should, just to see if it was as bad to watch as it was to play in. There was so much excitement before the game. It wasn't an FA Cup Final, but it was still a cup to go for, so it was a massive anti-climax. If we had either won or lost that day, I'm adamant the season would have turned out very different without the fixture backlog that it created.

The first replay was a better game, in Sheffield, and we almost won it at Hillsborough with a Roger Kenyon own goal ten minutes from time, until Bob Latchford scored for them to make it 1-1 in the 88th minute. Then we played out extra time still without a winner. I recall the players looking at each other thinking, 'What happens now? Have we really got to do this again?'

Of course, we did have to and the final match at Old Trafford was more exciting, at least for the supporters. Three goals in three minutes towards the end of the game was very out of character for this contest and when it looked like we were heading for unknown territory at 2-2 – who knew, possibly a fourth match – thankfully Brian Little stuck in the winner in the 119th minute. There was a feeling of relief more than elation at winning the cup. Their players probably felt the same.

It was fabulous to have won a cup and pick up a tankard (not a medal), but my overriding memory of this campaign is of what might have been, or even what should have been. We should have won the treble! When you walk off the pitch having blown away the best side in the world 5-1 as we had against Liverpool, you can't help thinking to yourself, 'Bloody hell, we're one hell of a team!' Which we were, on our day. We were good enough to have won the league. But not only that, we could also have won the FA Cup with the way we were playing. We ended up going out 2-1 in a quarter-final at Manchester United, the eventual winners that year, despite Brian putting us 1-0 up in the second minute. I'm convinced that in normal circumstances we would have seen that game out, even though we were missing Andy, Crops and Chris Nicholl on the day. We had played 120 minutes in yet another League Cup Final stalemate three days earlier. And that was four days after playing the initial final. I remember going into that match feeling a bit jaded and I imagine the other lads were also. We came off the pitch shattered and were distraught in the dressing room because we knew the FA Cup was there for the taking.

All in all, it was a successful campaign but nowhere near as good as it should have been. This should have been our first FA Cup win in 20 years, but instead the club is still waiting since 1957 for that moment of glory. And it should certainly have been my first league championship medal. We had to wait a bit longer for that!

Camp Nou to Camp Blues

*'Villa against Blues wasn't a football
match … they never came to play
football, they came to mess us about.
I honestly never enjoyed one game of
football in my Villa career against
Birmingham City'*

WE ALL hoped to kick on to great things after coming fourth and winning the League Cup, but we never quite managed it straight away. Ron was always tinkering with the squad to find the right balance and personnel and the summer of 1977 was a particularly seismic one with the players that came and went.

The big development was our captain Chris Nicholl being sold, to everyone's surprise, to Southampton. Chris had been a key player for us. It was quite ruthless of Ron to let him go when he was a fans' favourite and still only 31. But footballers are traditionally a selfish bunch. You might not particularly like it if one of your mates gets sold but ultimately you just want to make sure you're still in the team and on the payroll.

Anything beyond that is not really in your power. Ron was clearly impressed by what he had seen from Ken McNaught in those League Cup finals against us and saw him as Chris's younger replacement.

People have questioned some player sales and suggested it was about dressing room dynamics but I'm not so sure. Dressing rooms are interesting places and most lads are very different in their own personalities and routines. You're never going to get 11 guys with the same personalities – neither should you want that. For instance, Ron liked us in the dressing room by 2.30pm for a 3.00pm kick-off. By that I mean being game-ready, not still messing around organising tickets for family and friends. I liked to be at the ground for 1.45pm at the latest with my tickets sorted out on the gate. By 2.00pm I'd be into my preparation for the match with no outside distractions. Someone like Allan Evans, another new signing that summer, liked to limber up on the field early and get a feel for the atmosphere and the ground, wherever we were that day.

Generally, the dressing room was a quiet and reflective place. So, you can imagine how taken aback I was when I played for the England B team in Czechoslovakia and just as we were about to walk through the tunnel, Mick Lyons lets out this incredibly loud roar. I jumped out of my skin and thought, 'Fuckin' 'ell – what was that?' I had never encountered that before. But that's what I mean about dressing rooms, everyone is different. Maybe that's how Mick got himself motivated and what they expected of Mick in the Everton dressing room. At Villa, we'd give it the big 'Come on lads!' but that was about it. Most people were just focused on their game.

This was the summer Jimmy Rimmer came in to replace John Burridge. I was a fan of Budgie and couldn't say a bad word about his goalkeeping. I thought he was a miniature Peter Shilton. He was a bit on the small side, and I have a feeling Ron thought his lack of height would cost him goals at times and he clearly just rated Jimmy higher. Budgie was a real character also, while Jimmy was fairly quiet. Ron wasn't one for having too many characters in his team. He liked his players a bit more down to earth. Ultimately, Jimmy was an outstanding goalkeeper and nobody can doubt that his signing proved to be a great move for Villa.

John Gregory came in from Northampton Town but was a bit of an anomaly. I don't think Ron could work out where his best position was. To be fair to John, he was versatile and became known as a utility player and unfortunately once you get that label, players seem to be played all over the pitch and are never given the chance to settle in one role, which seemed to be the case for John at Villa. It wasn't until he moved on to Brighton and then QPR that he seemed to find his best position, which I think was in midfield. At Villa he probably played in every position apart from goalkeeper!

I don't think John's character enamoured him to the manager, though. John could be laissez-faire, cocky and full of himself, and he let himself down with his attitude. He was someone who seemed to enjoy being a footballer rather than someone who respected the authority and regimental routines of the job. I'm trying to be diplomatic, but I thought he was a bit of a prima donna. I liked John and got along with him, and the fact he ended up with six caps for England shows he was a quality player, but Ron wasn't having him for long.

Another who came and went quickly was Tommy Craig. It just never worked out for him. It was a bit of a dilemma for Ron as he had lost Alex Cropley with a broken leg, so brought in some experience with Tommy. But Gordon Cowans was coming through fast and it soon became clear Ron was favouring Gordon to Tommy, so he never stayed long and was eventually moved on to Swansea City. Tommy simply wasn't industrious enough for Ron. He tried to sit in at left midfield and dictate the game from there; he could pass the ball, but wasn't the greatest runner and Ron liked his midfielders to work their socks off. Now Alex and Gordon could pass the ball beautifully, but both were also industrious. It was just another example of how Ron was constantly adjusting the midfield to find the right balance. It wasn't until Des Bremner came to the club in 1979 that he was totally happy with it.

The most notable part of the 1977/78 campaign was our UEFA Cup run, which saw us progress to the quarter-finals. It took a Johan Cruyff-inspired Barcelona to stop us from winning that competition, I believe. It was there for the taking.

Turkish outfit Fenerbahce were our initial opponents and we made light work of them in the first round with 4-0 and 2-0 wins, home and away. Our potent strikeforce of Andy, 'Dixie' Deehan and Brian notched all six goals between them over both legs. It really makes a difference to a team when you have an attack that is as free-scoring as those guys were at that time. Turkish grounds are infamously volatile and although I don't remember their ground being all that big (with a 25,000 attendance), you always go to places like that intent on keeping the home fans quiet and we managed that.

I'd love to tell you tales of mischief and mayhem while we were on the road through Europe but that wasn't my style, being a non-drinker. I liked to prepare for a big match in the right way by going to bed at a decent hour. I probably pissed off a few room-mates who wanted to raid the mini-bar and chat till late, but it just wasn't my thing. My roomy used to be John Robson but his multiple sclerosis illness started to limit his appearances that season, so I found myself needing a new roomy. I had a habit of losing room-mates for reasons I just alluded to. My fellow Kirkby Boy Kenny Swain became a regular room-mate, while I recall Brian Little with Giddy and 'Big Ken' McNaught with Jimmy.

The second round against Gornik Zabrze was all about Ken McNaught. He'd had a hard time settling in at Villa until we played the Poles as nothing seemed to be going right for him. The manager backed his judgement and kept faith in him and we all believed in the manager. Ultimately, nobody plays the game to sabotage the team, you want to play well and win games and score goals if you can. So, when Ken scored both goals at home in a 2-0 win over Gornik the whole world seemed to lift from his shoulders and the fans who were giving him stick then started to see the player that Ron had seen when he brought him to Villa.

He came off the field as the hero and it was a nice lift for him. I noticed over the years there is always a minority of fans who, once they have a downer on you, always fail to see the good that you do. It doesn't matter what you do, they'll always see the negatives more than the positives. Maybe that's just the human nature of the football fan, and although not all are like that, you do get a good portion who are. Players have to accept that you'll never win everyone over. We saw the tie out with a 1-1 draw in Poland to progress to the last 16.

Perhaps a bigger indication of the upward curve we were on wasn't the European games we had come through to that point but the next game, three days after our trip to Gornik. We went to Anfield and beat Bob Paisley's Liverpool 2-1 thanks to two goals from Andy. They hadn't been beaten on their patch for 20 months having gone the whole of the 1976/77 season unbeaten at home. The last time they had been toppled at 'Fortress Anfield' was by Jack Charlton's Middlesbrough in March 1976. I should mention that our win against them came in a bizarre four-match losing streak they were on, but the other losses were all on the road. We didn't get carried away by that result – Ron would never have let us anyway – but it was just another example that we were heading in the right direction. Ron always saw Liverpool as the benchmark for where his teams were at, so we weren't doing too badly by those standards!

That was the first time I played against Liverpool with Kenny Dalglish in the side since he had replaced Kevin Keegan. I had seen him play for Scotland by then and knew he started his career south of the border with a bang (with six goals in his first eight games), but at the time his name wasn't on my radar. I certainly didn't go into that game worrying about Kenny Dalglish or being overly aware of his reputation. Maybe he became the new Messiah but that is not how I saw it. His sudden meteoric rise didn't surprise me, though, because Liverpool rarely made bad signings, generally. They always did their homework and research on players, better than any club in the country.

The next three results in the league showed why we were still some way from achieving sustained success when we lost 1-0 at home to our eternal bogey side Middlesbrough, then drew with Chelsea and lost at Ipswich. We even lost away to Middlesbrough the following month! I don't know why but we never seemed to be able to beat them. Even when we won the league in '81, we lost at Ayresome Park. It's so disappointing to look back on these results. I know there is absolutely nothing we can do about it now, but it still frustrates me that we pulled off what was a monumental result against the eventual European champions Liverpool and then flopped against Boro and a poor Chelsea team. If we could have taken two wins from those three games, we could have been challenging for the title along with Liverpool and Nottingham Forest. Those kinds of results, though, summed up why we weren't ready to challenge at that time and Ron knew it, hence the ongoing overhaul of the squad.

My first European goal, a rare header, helped us get through to the quarter-finals after toppling awkward opponents Athletic Bilbao. We eased through the home leg 2-0 and then drew one apiece in Spain. The reports before this tie were all about the fact Bilbao hadn't lost a home game in Europe for seven seasons. We were only a couple of minutes from spoiling that record, but the consolation was that we went toe to toe with them – and they were a very physical team. Their crowd clapped us off because they recognised how well we had played. Their ground was small and the crowd were on top of us and we really needed to dig deep to see that one through. It showed we had resilience as well as some footballing talent.

It was disappointing to draw Barcelona in the last eight because the standout player in Europe at that time was Cruyff and we knew we'd have to keep him quiet if we were to progress. I had played against some terrific players by this stage like Bobby Charlton, George Best and Franz Beckenbauer but none were better than Cruyff. He was their ringmaster, their conductor. He seemed like he was floating on air when he was on the ball. His pace was amazing, while he also created panic just from his footballing intelligence.

Cruyff was supposed to be up front but would drop into the midfield and would be unmarked and you'd start panicking about who would leave their man to pick him up. It was very clever play – he knew what he was doing. The central defenders considered coming out of defence to pick him up but knew that would then leave a huge hole in the defence, which was, of course, what he wanted. Invariably, it was a midfielder who marked him, but it was pointless as you couldn't get anywhere near him.

We played at Villa Park first. Ron used his best efforts to keep us calm and prevent us from concentrating on Cruyff too much by looking at their team sheet in the dressing room and pretending to pronounce his name wrong before screwing up the team sheet and throwing it across the room. That was Ron saying, 'Johan who?' It was irrelevant though as he ran the show and was subbed off after helping put them 2-0 up with just under ten minutes left. Somehow, we scrambled two late goals through Dixie and Big Ken and earned a spirited 2-2 draw. We had something to take to the Camp Nou. I have no doubts that if he didn't come off, we would have lost that game as nobody could get near him.

Before we went to Barcelona for the second leg, I played in a testimonial match for the referee Jack Taylor. It was an England XI against a Midlands XI at Villa Park. We had the likes of Derek Statham, John Gidman, Brian Little, John Richards, Jim Montgomery, Bryan Robson and John Wile. The England players included Mervyn Day in goal, Phil Thompson, Mick Lyons, Steve Williams, David Fairclough, Alan Ball and Brian Talbot. It was nice to be involved in a friendly match against international-level opponents but was far from the full cap I was still striving for.

We went to Barcelona thinking we had a good chance, even though Ron had left Andy at home, which we later heard was against Andy's wishes and pissed him off enough for him to want to leave. Only in recent times did I learn that the decision by Ron was the reason Andy Gray wanted out of Villa. We still felt confident though as John Gidman was back in the side after missing the home leg. I thought John's ability to get forward and deliver dangerous crosses would give us a real threat. Unfortunately, John allowed them to wind him up, he got into a fight and was sent off after a reckless challenge. Only Giddy knows why he lashed out, but his sending off cost us badly and we ended up losing 2-1 after Brian Little had earlier put us in front. It was an opportunity missed and I think we all left the Camp Nou feeling that if we could have got past Barcelona, we would have gone on to win the UEFA Cup. We matched them for large periods and the fact they ended up losing to PSV Eindhoven in the semi-finals showed they were far from unbeatable. It was just nice to be able to play against Cruyff and at one of the world's great stadiums.

If our progress was steadily improving by then, what was starting to happen at Nottingham Forest was meteoric and they were a great inspiration to clubs like us that anything is possible. They got promoted to the top tier in 1977, then won the league championship at the first attempt and consecutive European Cups. It was incredible but it showed what could be achieved, even at a time when it seemed Liverpool were winning everything.

Brian Clough assembled a Forest squad whereby the target message was all about 'the team', which was very similar to the philosophy that our own manager Ron Saunders held. He never set out to buy superstars, though several of the players he bought did become that, like Peter Shilton and Trevor Francis. He wanted players who would buy into his hard-working vision. They also had a tremendous balance in their team. I remember John Robertson from when I played against him for Coventry's youth team. He had great ability and I admired how he could cross a ball with no space around him. We often spoke about that as a team, closing him down, but still he managed to get quality crosses in to the likes of Tony Woodcock, Garry Birtles and Peter Withe season after season.

The player who broke my heart though was Shilton. He was so good. You'd shoot and half-celebrate with your hands in the air before he would somehow get a hand on the ball and keep it out. He was amazing. We always struggled against Forest in that late 1970s period. Maybe Ron learned from them and was inspired by Cloughie, I don't know, as he had a firm idea himself of what he was looking for to take us to the next level.

One thing I know, we had great games of football against Forest, not like against the Blues!

It pains me to say it, but our bitter local rivals Birmingham City could also be something of a bogey team for us. They did the league double over us in both the 1976/77 and 1977/78 seasons, whereas we always seemed to beat our other closest rivals West Bromwich Albion. West Brom hated us like Blues but when Villa and the Baggies played, it was a football match. Yes, it could be a little nasty at times but generally it was a football match. They had a couple of assassins at the back with Ally Robertson and John Wile but elsewhere they had a lot of good footballers.

Villa against Blues wasn't a football match. We knew we had to roll our sleeves up when we played them and be ready for the fight because they never came to play football, they came to mess us about. I don't think that is doing them a disservice, that's how I genuinely remember the matches with them over the years that I was involved in. I honestly never enjoyed one game of football in my Villa career against Birmingham City. I always enjoyed the matches against West Brom and most other teams. Against Birmingham the games felt as though they were played at 100 miles an hour, you didn't have time to play. That's probably because everyone was conscious that if they dwelled on the ball, they were likely to get clattered or badly injured such was the nature of the tackles that would be flying in. You just didn't have time to get the ball down and pass it, so we never had the time to control a match against

Blues like we did against West Brom, who we scored a lot of goals against.

The Birmingham games were so much more difficult. There are some iconic moments that supporters will recall from the Villa–Blues derbies from this era, and not for the right reasons, I hasten to add. I would like to say the matches were better at some other moment in time but I thought they were always like this. There was a mentality about this fixture that contributed towards a real nasty atmosphere on and off the pitch. If there are two things that a Birmingham City fan wants every season – when the clubs are in the same league – it is to beat Villa, which is quite sad. I felt the way the Blues fans hated the Villa had an influence on the way the players approached these derbies. That mentality seems to have carried on ever since. We saw headbutt incidents between Noel Blake and Steve McMahon, then between Robbie Savage and Dion Dublin in more recent times, and the most violent of them all perhaps, when that Birmingham supporter ran on the pitch at St Andrew's and punched Jack Grealish in the head. So, with all this going on, is it any surprise that we could never really play our natural game?

I felt, though, playing at The Hawthorns had a more volatile atmosphere than at St Andrew's as the West Brom fans were even nastier towards us than the Blues fans. But for some reason we were able to play our football and beat them so therefore I enjoyed the games there more than I did against the Blues. I have a feeling that was because they made us walk through this tunnel with the crowd all over us and abusing us to the hilt, so by the time we got out onto the pitch we were quite psyched up ourselves and motivated to win. Even when I was at Coventry, I enjoyed my games at West Brom. Their fans did like to be entertained and it made for a better spectacle. The Ron Atkinson years were especially evident of that flamboyant attitude. Alex Cropley's broken leg came in a derby match against West Brom in December 1977, but it was ironic as there was no culpability on the part of Ally Brown. It was more to do with the way Alex went into challenges – he over-committed himself at times, but that can be symptomatic of a high-pressure derby.

On the topic of discipline, I should give mention to the only sending off in my career, which came at Carrow Road in December 1979. We scored early through Allan Evans and although we were coasting to a 1-0 win, it should have been 5-0, as we missed a hatful of chances. Then, two minutes from time, the referee blew for a Norwich penalty on the advice of the linesman. There was supposedly a foul, but it was nowhere near the area. I went ballistic at the linesman and was given a straight red for dissent. I can't remember what I said but I'm sure my language wouldn't have been pretty. There you go. Not something I'm proud of but one red in almost 20 years isn't bad.

I Was No Snitch

*'There was no way I was going to shake
Andy Gray's hand. I didn't even want to
be in his company'*

ANDY GRAY wrote in his 2004 autobiography *Gray Matters* that we weren't friends and that I was some kind of teacher's pet with Ron Saunders. That came as a huge surprise to me and pissed me off, as none of it is true. Again, in a more recent book on Aston Villa, *Ticket to the Moon*, Andy inferred that I was taking dressing room gossip and reporting it back to Ron. To be precise, he said this of me in his memoirs:

'He was a good player and a terrific captain, but I never got on with him. I always thought he was too close to Ron Saunders. He was the manager's eyes and ears in the dressing room and if anything got said, Saunders soon heard about it. Dennis and I clashed a few times in training at Villa. Then when I was

at Wolves, I was sent off for having a hack at
him in a derby match at Villa Park. I make
no excuses for that. But it didn't connect and
it was a one-off.'

Andy could not be more wrong. To make matters worse, John Gidman also said words to that effect in *Ticket to the Moon* and though he didn't name me it was obvious he was talking about me and referred to me as 'the snitch'. Let me tell you, I was never a snitch.

I was far more upset by Giddy talking about me like that because I thought we were good mates. It was totally against the relationship that we had. I guess he never liked me calling him greedy when he left Villa for more money, but I didn't like the way he blamed the manager for the reasons he left. I wanted to put the truth out there. I don't see any other reason why we fell out other than what went on in those last few months of his time at Villa. I found it distasteful for him to talk about the football club and the manager in the way he did.

A backdrop of boardroom tensions added to the whole situation. Both Andy and Giddy left Aston Villa in late 1979. First Andy made his debut for Wolves in the September after they paid a British record transfer fee of almost £1.5 million, then Giddy debuted for Everton a month later following his £650,000 move. I had been captain of Villa for a year by then – from the start of the 1978/79 season, after Ron had sold Leighton Phillips to Swansea City.

It was a shock for me at the time to be made captain, but once Leighton had departed, I guess Ron needed a leader from somewhere. I now know, thanks to a story told by then-secretary Alan Bennett, that Ron always saw captaincy material in me. I didn't have a clue of those plans at the time of course. I hadn't been a captain since I led the Coventry youth team but despite my lack of experience in leadership roles, this wasn't something I was ever going to turn down. It was a huge honour for me and I remained captain of the club for the next few years. I saw myself as a leader or spokesman of the players but didn't always put myself out there like some as I am not exactly outgoing or outspoken.

I wasn't a rah-rah captain and was someone who tried to lead by example more than giving loud, Churchillian speeches. There would be times in matches where I had to remind players of their responsibilities to the team. Someone like Colin Gibson wasn't averse to losing his temper and I might just rein him in otherwise we'd be down to ten men, so I saw things like that as part of my role. Other than that, I was just a player who wanted to do well for my team and lead by example, on and off the field. I never saw myself as Ron's eyes and ears in the dressing room. I never went into Ron's office in my life, unless I was called in there by Ron. Jimmy Rimmer had more of a relationship with Ron than I did.

By the time I became skipper, there was increasing disharmony in the boardroom and this was the time when chairman Bill Dugdale and his fellow directors Alan Smith and Harry Cressman resigned as they became tired of the treatment of Ron, who was building something exciting. Yet he always seemed to be at loggerheads with the board, or Doug Ellis more to the point, who was never averse to interfering in team matters. I still have newspaper cuttings from the time and one story suggested Ron might be off to Saudi Arabia because of his frustrations. I'm not sure how accurate that was but I know he was frustrated by Doug's interference. I was always loyal to Ron because he was the one who identified my talents at Coventry and brought me to Villa. Many other players would agree with me, but there were also those like John Gidman, Brian Little and Andy Gray who probably had more loyalty to Doug. Giddy and Brian, to be fair, had known Doug since they came through the ranks almost a decade earlier.

I didn't get involved in the politics but the director Harry Kartz called me, Jimmy and Ken McNaught into Ron's office at Bodymoor Heath one day, when Ron wasn't there. He wanted to gauge the feelings of the dressing room with everything that was going on because the negative media reports and internal lobbying was not good for the football club. What Harry was really trying to do was work out if we were on Doug's side or Ron's side. The added issues of Andy and Giddy were also adding to the whole situation and Harry wanted our view on everything, to see where we stood. We never talked or moaned about Andy or Giddy as their issues were not any of our business and we didn't mention Doug either, but what we did say was that we felt things were going in the right direction under the management of Ron. We felt the way forwards for Aston Villa was Ron Saunders.

We might have said that apart from two players who are unhappy, the rest of the squad want to get on with things and win matches for Aston Villa. We urged Harry to put an end to the negative talk and said the board needs to decide on what's going to happen, and we hoped the board would come out strongly in favour of Ron. That was our straightforward case in a nutshell. That's about as involved as I or any other player got in this saga, as far as I know. It's quite likely that if Doug had won that power struggle, Ron would not have been at Villa for long thereafter. It would also, therefore, have been interesting to know that if that scenario did play out, with Doug staying and Ron going, if Andy and Giddy would still have left. I suppose we will never know.

Despite what happened in the event, I will never allow those disappointing circumstances of the late 1970s to cloud some great memories. Andy and Giddy were a big part of that dream team in 1976/77 along with Brian Little, Alex Cropley, Frank Carrodus, Chris Nicholl and the rest of us. We really ought to have achieved more than just winning the League Cup. It was a fabulous team that played exhilarating football. It was an opportunity missed and, unfortunately, we lost our way for a couple of seasons following that campaign. Injuries didn't help and we barely fielded the same midfield two weeks running let alone the same XI. That lack of continuity cost us dearly.

The toxicity in the boardroom peaked by the time Giddy and Andy left. Doug was eventually ousted by the increasingly influential father and son directors Ronald and Donald Bendall, and Harry Kartz. Doug wanted to regain the power and chairmanship he had surrendered in 1975. The boardroom battle was monumental. Doug tried to use the fact that two of our biggest players were unsettled and had requested transfers as a way to sack Ron. Fortunately, the other directors backed Ron. Andy and Giddy had their own reasons for wanting away but it's common knowledge they didn't get along with Ron all that well, at least by that stage. Fortunately, the Bendalls, and indirectly Ron, came out victorious and the all-powerful Ronald Bendall subsequently gave Ron his full backing as manager.

It would have been a disaster for Aston Villa if Doug had won that power struggle. I can't be 100 per cent certain that we wouldn't still have won trophies if Doug had won, but the club would have been far less likely to have won the league championship and European Cup like we did while he was away from Villa Park between 1979 and 1982. It's quite likely, though, that Ron Saunders wouldn't have been manager and instead Doug would have brought in players that I would call circus clowns, or at least bigger names who were all about themselves, rather than winning matches. When I say clowns, I don't mean that in a derogatory sense, I mean talented footballers but who appeared to like to entertain and show off more than they liked to focus on winning games.

Ron didn't like show-offs. I was told that when Ron bought me, Doug had tried to persuade him to buy Rodney Marsh instead. Ron had already managed Rodney at Manchester City and wasn't too impressed then and wasn't about to sign him as Villa manager. Ron didn't like stars or larger-than-life characters. The only star we ever had in our team was Andy Gray but even that was out of Ron's development after he signed him from Dundee United. Doug's typical signings were Didier Six, David Ginola and Stan Collymore. I'm not saying they weren't great players, but they were individuals and not necessarily great for the team.

There has been talk that preceding that boardroom vote, players took sides and were either on Doug's side or they were with Ron Saunders (and the Bendalls). I never took any sides though I was always loyal to Ron. I had no interest in political stuff like that and didn't get involved, but what I didn't like were the stories coming out in the press. Andy commented that under Ron's management the club would never win anything. Personal disputes or issues between Andy and Ron were between them, but I felt in saying we would never win anything under Ron, it was also a slight on the players. So, I thought he had crossed a line there. I never confronted any player for wanting to leave because you know and accept as a player there will always be footballers who will come and go. I saw that early on at Coventry. It's just part of the game.

I couldn't understand why Andy wanted to go to Wolves, though. That was a downward move for him, no doubt. Wolves were struggling and were only two places above the relegation zone the season before. I was under the impression he wanted to better himself and win things, so I was surprised he chose Wolves. As it turned out they won the League Cup in 1980 so fair play to him, but his next move was better for him, when he went to Everton and they had a purple patch.

Before he left, though, I felt it was my role as captain to redress the balance and I spoke up for Ron and us as a team. I didn't want the fans to think we all felt the same way and there was disunity in the dressing room because that wasn't the case. If players came out and said they wanted to get away, my sentiments were, 'Why do you want to get away? What's the motivation?' I'm aware Andy fell out with Ron over him being left out at the Camp Nou and subsequent comments Ron made about Andy. The only comments I made publicly at that time, which might have been viewed badly by Giddy and Andy, were along the lines of the players are together and I didn't want anyone hiding behind excuses for leaving. I wanted more truth.

Giddy almost certainly wanted more money. I don't believe he had a major issue with Ron because he had played well for him for five years before he left. The same is true to a lesser extent with Andy.

We were all on a leash as players and had standards we were expected to live up to. But Giddy had the longest leash of all of us at the club in terms of what he said and how he conducted himself at times. John's story of his first meeting with Ron, as told in *Ticket to the Moon*, summed up what he felt about authority and the people he was working for. Ron being Ron asked him in his office, 'Who are you?' Then Giddy said, 'Well, who the fuck are you?'

Giddy would come into training on some days and you'd wonder where he had been. Nobody in the dressing room asked him, but you can bet your bottom dollar that Ron knew. Ron gave Giddy more leeway than any other player as long as he did his training and played well. Ron let things slide, despite Giddy's criticisms of him. My old mate Terry McDermott liked a drink and Bob Paisley often looked the other way with him as long as his performances were of a particular standard on matchdays and as long as he wasn't embarrassing the club. Ron was a lot more of a players' man than he is given credit for.

I wasn't sorry when John left in the end because I felt let down by his nonsense to want to get away, jumping on the bandwagon with Andy. I was more disappointed by the departure of Andy. If I had the choice of one of them staying, I would have said Andy because he was a proven goalscorer and goalscorers like that are not easy to replace.

Ron sold several players because they were probably too much of a character for him like Jake Findlay, Bobby McDonald, John Gregory, John Burridge and more. But Ron also showed that if players who you might term as mavericks were in his team and doing what he wanted them to, like Giddy and Brian Little, he was happy to live with their quirks or character differences that he didn't like. Same with Andy. What manager would be happy to let one of his players invest money in a nightclub, which is what Andy did? Andy might say it was none of Ron's business what he did with his money outside of Aston Villa, but if that was Fergie at Manchester United, he would never have allowed his players to be involved in nightclub ownership. But Ron used it to motivate Andy. He was a shrewd psychologist. On the opening night of the club he said to Andy, if we're winning at half-time and you're playing well, I'll sub you off and you can get changed early and go and open your club. What (other) manager would say that?

How Giddy and myself fell out is disappointing and a surprise to me really because we were two Liverpool boys playing together in the same team. In fact, me and my wife and Giddy and his wife ended up in the Algarve together on holiday one summer. They asked us where we were going and then booked themselves onto the same holiday. We were glad to have them join us as we were good team-mates and our wives got on well. The only thing I didn't like was that Giddy booked a beautiful villa with a swimming pool and we had an apartment in the middle of the town, with no pool and the sound of motorbikes going up and down all day and night! He really outdid me there, did John. Fair play to him, I only wish he had booked mine as well! We never had any problems.

It was the same story with Andy. We got along fine and were good mates along with the likes of Frank, Gordon Smith, Alex and Brian. We would take our wives and girlfriends up to Andy's club, Holy City Zoo, on a Saturday night. There was never a problem. I never felt like anything other than a big friend of Andy Gray. So, it really shocked me when I read in his book that we weren't friends. I don't know why Andy said that as we never had a problem on or off the pitch.

I have no idea how myself, Andy and Giddy went from being team-mates and friends off the field to them calling me a dressing room snitch. It's sour grapes. I would like to know the amount of times John knocked on the manager's door because I can tell you it would be a lot more than what I did, usually for a pay rise. John's motivation was money, my motivation was not money, it was playing football and winning trophies in the knowledge that if I did both of those things, the money would come. John always wanted to be on more money than anyone else. But listen, he ended up getting his move and probably earned a lot more money. You have to say Giddy ended up having a great career at Villa and afterwards playing for three more big clubs in Everton, Manchester United and Manchester City. He won the FA Cup at Wembley with United, he got an England cap as well, so he should be very happy with his career. Only he can tell you the truth as to why he is still so bitter about me and his time at Villa, because I can tell you it has nothing to do with any conversations I had with Ron.

It is even more disappointing to me that whatever went on in 1979 between myself, Andy and Giddy – and as I have explained I didn't even think we had fallen out – that time has not been a healer. The fact both have carried so much bitterness through the years is surprising and disappointing.

The club put on a function in 2007 to celebrate three anniversaries: 50 years since winning the FA Cup in 1957; 30 years after the League Cup in 1977; and it was also the 25th anniversary of us winning the European Cup, so I featured in two of those teams. We all met in a room at Villa Park at the start of the night for the initial reception and I made sure I stayed at the other end of the room to Andy Gray. I didn't like what he had said about me in his book and I was intent on keeping my distance. There was no way I was going to shake his hand. I didn't even want to be in his company. He had a lot of people around him and was the centre of attention anyway, so he probably didn't notice I was staying away. The only way I would have spoken to him would have been if he had come over to me to apologise, but he didn't. As we were leaving the room to go to the dinner, though, he walked past me and grabbed my hand and shook it, so he did shake my hand but there was no apology or anything else.

Later that evening, the 1977 team was on stage and I was being interviewed by Nick Owen. I happened to mention the successful team that Ron Saunders had put together and as soon as I said 'Ron Saunders' I saw Giddy walk off the stage. People noticed that and felt it was a slight against me, but I always thought it was Giddy's protest against Ron. Maybe it was a combination of both? I thought it was distasteful and led to other people commentating on the situation and probably getting the wrong end of the stick. It's all a great shame.

Liverpool Were Taking the Piss

'I looked at their players casually throwing this trophy around and it pissed me off … I felt quite angry … I told myself some other team needs to win that trophy and that we would be in their position next year and show it means more to us'

I HAVE a confession to make.

When we were at Anfield for the last game of the 1979/80 season, I had a glimpse of the future while I was sitting in the stands with a thigh strain that had sidelined me for the last few weeks of that campaign. Despite being roundly beaten 4-1 and even though we had a few rookies in the side like Brendon Ormsby, Noel Blake, Pat Heard, Ivor Linton and, to a lesser extent, Dave Geddis, I had this premonition. A premonition that we would win the league championship the following season. That vision would probably have caused a chuckle amongst many pundits then, had I made my thoughts public, given we finished seventh in the league. It certainly wasn't our performance on the day that influenced me, though I knew we weren't that far behind them as we had a lot of key players out in the match. We had beaten a full-strength Liverpool 3-1 at home a year earlier, so there were encouraging signs.

The thing that really motivated me to win the league the next season and which really made me think we could, was watching the Liverpool players celebrate with the league championship trophy on the pitch after that game (their fourth league title in five years, with Nottingham Forest snapping their winning streak in 1978). I looked at their players casually throwing this trophy around and it pissed me off. I thought, 'Is that what it's all about, winning the league?' It almost looked like it didn't mean that much to them because they were so accustomed to winning the league every season.

Knowing those fabulous players as I do, I am positive it meant an awful lot to them, but on that day, everything just looked so blasé as if they knew they would win the league – again. I wasn't having it, I thought they were taking the piss and I felt quite angry and I wanted winning the league to mean much more. I thought, 'It's our time.' I told myself at that point some other team needs to win that trophy and that we would be in their position next year and show that it means more to us. It obviously did because we hadn't won it for 71 years. I guess when you are so used to winning these huge trophies all the time it is easy for it to look like it doesn't mean as much. I didn't tell anyone about that premonition, but I also didn't think it was unachievable.

Liverpool were quite fortunate on that day because we put out half of our reserves. If we had won that day and if Manchester United had won (and not lost) at Leeds, Liverpool would have been runners-up to United. So, while they were a fantastic team, they weren't always running away with it. But I guess finding a way to win trophies time after time is not a coincidence, it was a habit they were used to.

The initial prelude to our most successful season in a generation came in the shape of one last team-rebuilding exercise from Ron Saunders. He was never averse to making ruthless decisions in terms of letting players go or signing players with little or no track record in the league. That was clear again in the summer of 1979.

John Gidman and Andy Gray were the big two outgoings as I have already discussed. He surprisingly sold John Deehan to West Brom, which shocked a few of us as Dixie was only 22 and scoring goals quite consistently. John Gregory left for Brighton, which was less of a surprise. Not because John wasn't a good player, but he just wasn't Ron's type with regards to his character. Injuries caught up with Frank Carrodus and he left us. Gordon Smith also departed for Tottenham and that left-back position was a bit of a problem. Initially, Ron tried to replace him with the experienced Mike Pejic, though he was troubled by injury for most of his two years at Villa. That's when the rookies

Gary Williams and Colin Gibson were given their opportunity and eventually showed they could fill that role for us. Kenny Swain had by now settled in well at Villa and Ron's masterstroke of moving him from right-winger to right-back was inspired and meant he didn't need to buy a new right-back to replace Giddy. The Allan Evans and Ken McNaught central defensive partnership was flourishing, while myself and Gordon Cowans welcomed a new midfield partner in 1979 in the shape of the little-known Des Bremner.

We didn't know much about Des, and he probably knew even less about us, but he soon showed that he was the perfect replacement for the industrious Frank Carrodus. I soon came to see that Des had all the same qualities as Frank but was a younger version. Des was better at challenging for the ball, and what he had over Frank was that extra tenacity in the tackle and then the ability to take the ball on and set up an attack. He was a bit like a right-sided Alex Cropley. As a bloke, Des was like me, not a big drinker with any notions of going nightclubbing. He got on with the game and felt the physicality he needed on the pitch would be better achieved by clean living. I played in the middle of the three of us, with Gordon to my left and Des to my right, but unlike the common perception I wasn't much of a ball-winner, that was more Des. He was a terrific professional.

We never knew what Ron was up to with regards to scouting players or his transfer plans. The only time he spoke to me about a player he was looking to bring in was Dave Geddis. He told me he hoped he might be able to eventually take over from Andy. It never worked out like that, but Dave still proved himself a decent signing who did a good job for us. The other major signing of that time was dynamic winger Tony Morley from Burnley, though injury meant we didn't get to see the best of him until the 1980/81 season. The young Brummie Gary Shaw, meanwhile, was starting to get more games after Andy left, especially with Brian Little struggling more and more through injury.

It was clear to everyone, though, that Ron was looking for someone to take Andy's place, which was never going to be easy as Andy had played such a significant part for us in all that we had done over the last few seasons. We heard years later that he wanted my old team-mate Mick Ferguson from Coventry but a disagreement over the transfer fee meant he ended up putting in a successful bid of £500,000 to Newcastle for Peter Withe.

Andy and Peter were very similar players. It's clear we wouldn't have needed Peter if Andy hadn't left, so it's not unthinkable to consider we could still have won the league championship and European Cup with Andy Gray and Gary Shaw up front as they were very much alike. But it wasn't to be. I was just pleased we signed Peter because the way I wanted to play was to hit a target-man type of player like him, and like Andy had been, and then play off them further up the field. Gordon Cowans was now developing into a world-class midfield player and with Tony Morley on the wing sending in quality crosses, what more could a centre-forward want? Peter did his homework to choose us over his boyhood team Everton and knew he was joining a team that was ready for success.

Peter came to Villa with a reputation as a journeyman having played for lots of clubs but a good journeyman who had tasted success, notably winning the league at Nottingham Forest. He soon proved himself to be exactly the player we needed, who linked up with the midfield or his strike partner and created chances for others as well as being able to finish himself. His partnership with Gary Shaw quickly flourished and they helped each other become better players. Peter, quite simply, was just the player we needed to make us tick again.

The one downside for me before that historic season of 1980/81 began was the FA Cup quarter-final upset that we suffered at West Ham late on in the previous campaign. It was another 'what if' story for me as far as the FA Cup went. I really believe we should have won the cup that year, but we came unstuck after a Ray Stewart penalty two minutes from the end. Anyone that followed football through that era will know that Ray rarely missed from the penalty spot. But my issue with the goal is that it shouldn't have been a penalty in the first place. Ken McNaught was adjudged to have handled a Trevor Brooking corner after an aerial challenge with Alvin Martin. The boss said on television afterwards that he watched it back 12 times but still couldn't see any conclusive evidence that

Ken had handballed on purpose. We probably spent five minutes arguing with the referee but as we all know, that never gets you anywhere. It was a big blow to go out like that.

It was never an easy game at Upton Park because it felt like the most intimidating ground in the country with the crowd so close to you. They went on to win it that year after beating Arsenal in the final but it's still hard not to think 'that should have been our year'. It was typical of my career as far as the FA Cup went. When I was at Coventry we lost to Wolves in the sixth round, or quarter-final, and I lost three quarter-finals with Villa, with this one at West Ham, plus Manchester United in 1977 and at Arsenal in 1983. Missed opportunities!

This is Why I Play Football

I BELIEVED we could win the league as soon as we beat Leeds at Elland Road in the first game of the season.

I saw what we were capable of. I thought to myself if we can sustain our fitness, physicality, energy, that fluent style of football and also remain strong with the mental side of the game, we were ready to win this league.

We just looked equipped. Myself, Des and Swainy were now 28 and had been around, Withey was 29 and had won a league title with Forest already, Jimmy at 32 was superb in goal and a steadying influence, Tony 26, Big Ken 25, while amongst that experience was a crop of vibrant young players who had proved to Ron they were ready. Shawsy was 19, Gibbo and Gary Williams 20, Sid (Cowans) not quite 22 and Evo (Allan Evans) was almost 24. The blend of youth and experience was perfect. It's true we were fortunate with injuries to be able to field only 14 players all season, which gave us good continuity, but we deserved that luck. Our injuries for the couple of seasons prior really took their toll and set us back. This time we were able to field seven ever-presents.

We were off to a flying start by winning five of our first six games. Even in the match we drew, at Manchester City, we were 2-0 up with ten minutes left so it should really have been a perfect start.

Fittingly, our first loss of this campaign was a 1-0 defeat at Ipswich Town. We ended up having a real ding-dong with them for the title and their players will be very quick to tell you they beat us three times that season – home and away in the league and in the FA Cup as well. I thought at the start of the season they would be the ones we would need to finish above if we were going to win the league. That might sound strange as Liverpool were the reigning champions, but I just thought we could beat Liverpool on a good day and Ipswich were building something special under Bobby Robson. There is no denying that Ipswich had a stronger squad than we did – they had more depth. They were clearly the darlings of the London press and it seemed to us that all the high-profile journalists wanted them to win the league. Maybe Ron Saunders just did a great Fergie-style siege mentality job on us, but this is how I remember it. That was fine with us and we were happy to be the underdogs and just fly beneath the radar of the national media, until they realised we were going to be challenging. Ipswich were stuffed with internationals, we weren't, but I certainly never felt inferior to them at any point. It was a real gunfight until the death all season.

At Portman Road on the first Saturday in September, we more than matched them and I actually felt we deserved to win, but a Frans Thijssen goal clinched the two points for them. Thijssen was a wonderful player and with those sparrow legs he reminded me of the great Johan Cruyff. Thijssen was so hard to win the ball off and would do these 360 turns yet still come away with the ball.

Both teams were probably quite similar in how they played. Their ball manipulator and conductor was Arnold Muhren in the same way that Gordon Cowans was for us. They had a big man up front in Paul Mariner, like we had Withey, with Eric Gates playing off him as Gary Shaw did for us. Tony Morley was a dynamic winger for us and they had Alan Brazil buzzing around from wing to wing, turning up in dangerous positions. John Wark was a fantastic, vital player for them and scored lots of goals from midfield – in a way that we didn't if I'm honest. We both also had settled central defensive partnerships – England duo Terry Butcher and Russell Osman for them and Ken and Evo for us. Both sides also had underrated English goalkeepers, though at least Jimmy won an England cap, which was one more than Paul Cooper. So, there were a lot of similarities, not to forget the two excellent managers.

We remained in the top two all season, once we beat our old rivals Birmingham City at St Andrew's in October. Tony Morley receives a lot of plaudits for his goal of the season at Everton in this campaign and rightly so, but I would also like to mention Allan Evans' winning goal at Birmingham. It was comfortably one of the goals of the season for me and nobody ever talks about it. Ken McNaught floated in a free kick from the halfway line and it missed everyone until Evo swivelled and smashed it into the roof of the net with his left foot on the half-volley. It was not only a fantastic goal but was such a significant win that kept us on our good run. Without the quality that we had in the team, the quality of Evans and Morley and others, we wouldn't have won those tight games. The other significant aspect to that goal, and the season as a whole, was it was yet another victory in a local derby. We had 14 local derbies – we won 11 and drew three. That was a huge factor in our success that season. Ipswich had two local derbies – against Norwich – and they drew one and lost one.

Everything wasn't always rosy in 1980/81. I remember, despite the magnificent run we were on, hitting a sticky patch before Christmas that meant we had to ask a few harsh questions of ourselves. Between our wins at Carrow Road in late November and at Villa Park against Stoke on Boxing Day, we won just one game in six. We lost at Anfield to a late Kenny Dalglish goal and lost games we should have won at Brighton and Middlesbrough.

We sat in the dressing room at the Goldstone Ground after that Brighton match and had a heart to heart. The boss reminded us about the great opportunity we had in front of us. Ron was never one for huge speeches, dishing out bollockings or looking beyond the next match, so I guess you could call it something of a reset. We were on a tough run and he just wanted to put things into perspective that we were still a good team and needed to get back to what we had been doing a few games before. We had a lot of experience and character in the dressing room and Ron would often sit back and let us police ourselves as far as what we needed to do. Most of his work was done on the training ground in midweek and he never ranted or raved at us in a dressing room.

This was and still is a tough league and that's why I said previously that if you're not on your game mentally you can come unstuck against any team. Brighton, for instance, might well have narrowly escaped relegation that season but they had some bloody good players with the likes of Mark Lawrenson, Michael Robinson, Steve Foster, Brian Horton, Gary Stevens and our old mate John Gregory. If you're not totally on your game, these guys let you have it. I don't want to make excuses but we were without Peter Withe at Middlesbrough and Brighton and we definitely missed him because Peter had a command of centre-halves. He could boss a game and was a huge presence for us. That's not a slight against Dave Geddis, who would come in and do a good job for us, but we had to play differently when

Dave was in the team and hit balls over the top for him to run onto – and that style didn't always suit us.

That honest moment of reflection might just have served its purpose because we never lost another league match until the middle of March at White Hart Lane. Our only defeat was in the FA Cup to Ipswich. From that game we won seven on the bounce but still we were only occupying the runner-up spot as Ipswich were on an equally impressive run (they didn't lose between mid-December and mid-March) so we kept pushing one another all season.

I always felt the real league championship title contenders in this season were us and Ipswich, but Liverpool still deserved huge respect as the reigning champions and they were actually top of the table when we went into our second match of the season against them in January, with us and Ipswich neck and neck behind them. Purely and simply, this game with the Reds was a showdown. They had been the team to beat for a few years, but this match was our moment to show we were not in a false position, we were there on merit and were ready to grab their crown off them. We lost at Anfield a couple of months earlier but only to a very late goal. There could be no excuses on this day, we had to win – and, of course, we didn't disappoint!

It was a pulsating encounter between two great teams. Remember, they won the European Cup in 1981, so they were far from a spent force even though they ended up finishing fifth and nine points behind us. It just puts our own achievements in perspective.

Withey put us 1-0 up by half-time and then I scored the goal in the 82nd minute that I had always dreamed of scoring against Liverpool.

It was the goal that not only put us 2-0 up and sealed the match but was possibly the most iconic goal of our season. It typified the way we played: counter-attacking with pace and fluency after working tigerishly to win the ball. Des Bremner's sliding tackle on their advancing left-back Alan Kennedy won the ball back for us and he knocked it to our own rampaging full-back Kenny Swain. He charged down the right and back-heeled it to Gary Shaw, whose measured pass split their defence to find me running through from midfield. I managed to slot the ball past Ray Clemence to the delight of a jubilant Holte End.

We had arrived! That goal typified what I enjoyed doing more than anything else, running through from deep, making it hard for defenders to pick me up. I don't think it's big-headed to say that goal is in Villa folklore and remains one of our most famous as a club, purely because it was a great team effort, the significance of the goal and who it was against. That game gave us the belief we were champions elect, even though there was still a long way to go. It was only January after all. Typically, Ron didn't get too excited as was his way. The boys were cock-a-hoop in the changing room, though, and we enjoyed that win, but as far as Ron was concerned it was a case of, 'Well done lads, but don't forget, it's Coventry away next Saturday.'

The Liverpool performance set us on our way to a seven-match winning run in the league and our confidence was through the roof. During that run I returned to my stomping ground to score a goal at Goodison Park, similar to the one I scored against Liverpool, but understandably Tony's goal of the season is all that most people remember of that match. But I certainly wouldn't begrudge him any praise as it was a cracker and again symbolic of some free-flowing exchanges between the lads to set him up.

We met up again with our old friends from Ipswich in the April and by this stage the national media were reporting that the league title was between us and them. Privately, we always got the feeling they were desperate for Bobby Robson to win it. Maybe he was more quotable that Ron Saunders? Ron was never bothered about being popular in the media, though. The build-up to that match was just like any other as far as we were concerned. For whatever reason though we didn't do ourselves justice on the night and lost 2-1. They celebrated quite hard in the away dressing room and we felt they thought they'd won the league. Maybe some of our players did, too, but as soon as we heard Ron's fighting spirit in his now infamous television interview, we were ready to take this fight to the wire. In response to a question about whether it now seemed to be Ipswich's title to lose, Ron retorted, 'Would you like to bet against us?' Game on.

We did everything we could to stay in the fight for the title and by the time of our last game of the season on Saturday, 2 May, we knew we had to win at Arsenal to be sure of the championship. Not much went right for us that day, though.

You couldn't make it up but our preparation for the most important match of our careers to date got off to the worst possible start when our team bus was stuck in miles of traffic on the M1 driving down to London. It looked like we would miss the kick-off at one point as we never had a police escort or anything like that. The driver opted to take the law into his own hands to help us out and drove on the hard shoulder for tens of miles just to get us to Highbury in time. We found out later there was a rugby union final at Twickenham that same day between Leicester Tigers (including Clive Woodward and Dusty Hare) and Gosforth in the John Player Cup. It certainly never helped our cause, logistically.

On reflection, it was bad planning. We would have been better off travelling down the day before, which was how we usually prepared for long-distance away games. Ron never got much wrong with our preparation but he could have managed this situation better. It's probably the only time I could say that. He thought having a night at home with our families would help to keep us more relaxed and not make us too nervous. But we would have been so much better going to London on the Friday, the day before.

There were over 57,000 fans packed into a sold-out Highbury. The crowd was amazing, especially the Villa fans who travelled down in their thousands. I'm just gutted we couldn't have given them the performance we all wanted to win the league with. We saved probably our worst display of the season for this day. Jimmy was at fault for the first goal by Willie Young, as the ball rolled under him despite it being quite a weak shot. Jimmy didn't make many mistakes, though, so no one would have blamed him. Their second was even worse. Kenny Swain got himself into a bit of a tangle on the edge of our area after a long through-ball and he allowed Brian McDermott to turn him. Even though Colin Gibson tried to cover, Brian McDermott was still able to see his bobbling shot find the far corner, past Jimmy's outstretched hand. It was another very poor goal to concede.

Fortunately, just when we needed a hero, up stepped Yugoslav striker Bozo 'Bosko' Jankovic. He saved us at Ayresome Park as his two goals cancelled out Paul Mariner's early strike as Middlesbrough beat Ipswich 2-1. It meant we were champions despite them having a game in hand on us. For what it's worth, they ended up losing that game in hand at home to Southampton and well and truly blew up, having lost four of their last five league games. Their consolation came in the shape of the UEFA Cup, which they won. But the league championship was ours.

I knew we had won the league before our match at Arsenal was finished just from the behaviour of our fans. It seemed clear that events were going our way at Middlesbrough. They were celebrating wildly and almost encroaching onto the pitch, ready to charge on.

I wasn't thinking about Ipswich as I was in a game, but with maybe five minutes to go, I started to hear fans shouting things like, 'Ipswich are losing' and 'You've won it'. I knew we had to get off that pitch sharpish as soon as that final whistle went, otherwise we would never make it to the dressing room, which was how it panned out. We were running down the tunnel and random people were shouting, 'You've won it, Ipswich have lost.' We got into the dressing room and waited for confirmation that the rumours were true, just as everyone else made it in from the crowded pitch. Ron came in with assistant Roy MacLaren and they confirmed it was all over. We were champions of England.

Ron rarely showed any emotion and even here, in his best moment, he just had a big grin on his face. There are plenty of photographs to show how happy he was at that moment. We're sitting together sharing a drink on a few of them; these are memories I treasure dearly. I wasn't a drinker but I allowed myself a few glasses of champagne that day – it was such a great celebration. To go 42 games, week in and week out, and then know you have come out on top ahead of so many great players at other top clubs, it really is the best feeling in the world.

I sat there for a moment, amidst the mayhem and celebrations, and reflected. 'This is why I play football,' I thought. 'This is why I wanted to play football for a living, to come away with winners' medals, to win trophies.' I recalled how I had personally set this very target in my head a year earlier having watched Liverpool collect the trophy at Anfield and celebrate with such abandon. It was now our time. Those were my personal thoughts but I also then thought of what it meant to the football club and to the supporters, having gone 71 years without winning this title. It was such a big deal.

The one downside was not being able to get our hands on the trophy that day and be able to celebrate with the fans during the moment. My original hope was to win at Stoke City and celebrate with the trophy at Villa Park after beating Middlesbrough in our penultimate match. That was my hope but in reality, we drew at Stoke and had to go to Arsenal needing a win to be sure.

We were presented with the trophy the next morning at the indoor Aston Villa Leisure Centre, before we went on an open-top bus parade through the streets of Birmingham city centre, where thousands of our fans turned out to welcome and cheer us, before a celebration at the Town Hall. I don't think the celebrations actually stopped between finishing the game at Highbury the day before and receiving the trophy on Sunday morning. For us more sensible ones, we got home and had a good night's sleep first. Apologies for the lack of drunken, tall tales of what we got up to. That wasn't my style. Maybe it's why I was captain!

When Birmingham City and Football Association official Jack Wiseman presented us with the trophy and medals, the late Eamonn Deacy was telling us all he didn't deserve a medal and would not collect one (he played nine games that season including sub appearances). I told Eamonn there were 16 medals yet only 14 players featured all season, so 'Go and get your medal, you deserve it as much as any of us.' All the lads also got on to him to take his medal. He did get his medal in the end but he took some persuading. I don't know who claimed the other two medals, but I think it was Ron Saunders and Roy MacLaren. I understand Tony Barton never got one, which was probably harsh on him given the contribution he made to our success. I loved the celebrations with my team-mates, but my period of celebration was controlled. When that Town Hall function was over, I went home as most of the other family men did. I'm sure the younger lads, or the unmarried lads, carried on and celebrated hard elsewhere – and so they should. It was well deserved!

The club then arranged a trip to California for us in and around Los Angeles. I would have preferred a shorter flight to somewhere like mainland Spain or Majorca, staying at a nice peaceful hotel in the summer sun with a chilled pool. Typical of the club then, what we got was a low-level, two-storey courtyard-style motel on the side of a busy road where the swimming pool wasn't even in operation. The pool was at the back, but there was no water in it. The hotel staff told us they weren't filling the pool up for another two weeks! So, there we were, stood around this empty swimming pool in boiling hot weather saying, 'Why the fuck has the club booked us into a hotel where there's no pool?'

The hotel fudged some excuse and said we could travel to their sister hotel further up the highway but I don't think anyone did. We mostly went sightseeing instead. I didn't have kids at the time so me and Jan generally socialised with Swainy, Spinksy (Nigel Spink), Evo, Des and their families. We hired this huge stationwagon and went to places like Universal Studios and toured round places like Beverly Hills looking at the houses of the rich and famous. It was a nice, seven-day break.

But before long we started to think about the following season and what we might be able to achieve next.

Reality Bites

'[Finishing 11th] wasn't good enough for a club that was on the verge of winning the European Cup … It comes down to the fact that our squad, ultimately, wasn't good enough … the results don't lie'

THERE WAS something very different about the new season. For a start, the wild beard that had given Jimmy Greaves reason to christen me the 'Flying Hippie' in his newspaper column was no more. That beard is part of Aston Villa folklore, I guess, because it's synonymous with me and the league championship trophy. But for the new season, I opted for a change. It was nothing to do with fashion, I simply liked the beard and felt it kept me a bit warmer in the colder months. But now the new season was upon us, it was time to get the razor out! The last time I did it I kept the moustache but, looking back, I wish I never.

The 1981/82 season was always going to be tougher than we had known for a long time. Firstly, because we were in the European Cup against the big clubs of the continent, which was a challenge Villa had never faced before. Secondly, because we were the champions of England and there would be plenty of clubs determined to take our crown off us, such as a wounded Liverpool and the bridesmaids of the previous league campaign, Ipswich. We knew we were going to be tested and we had to be ready.

Ron only made one signing in the summer. I didn't know much about 21-year-old Andy Blair, who came in from Coventry City, but we knew he was a midfielder. I did think, 'Well, where's he going to play?' Tony Barton had a great eye for talent, so we always trusted his judgement. Looking back now, we probably needed more quality bringing in to add depth to the squad than just Andy as we had been fortunate with injuries in 1980/81. In all honesty, at the time I didn't think we needed more players as we had quality youngsters at the club. I hoped they would start to come through and establish themselves along with the senior players who were already in the team. I thought if we could keep the continuity that we had and if players like Peter Withe weren't silly by getting booked too much and being suspended, we would be fine.

Shawsy, for instance, had just enjoyed the season of his dreams and he was only going to get better. Peter wasn't going to get better because he was already at his best but his partnership with Gary certainly could keep improving and that excited me. We also had the likes of Brendon Ormsby and Terry Donovan, who were pushing the first-team players, so I didn't have a problem with where our squad was then. We were still a team that could cause any side in the league a problem – we just didn't do that often enough during our title defence.

The squad wasn't helped by the forced retirement, due to injury, of Villa hero Brian Little. It must have been so disheartening for Brian to be part of our squad and to have to watch from the sidelines as we won the league championship. He clearly didn't know what was going to happen to him through that season but I'm sure he hoped he was going to come back. To have had Brian back fit in that squad and able to come in for Shawsy if we ever needed to make a change, it would have made such a big difference to the quality of our squad. Brian would have hit it off well with Peter as he was used to playing with a big target man from his time with Keith Leonard and then Andy Gray.

Brian's retirement was a massive disappointment for us because he still had an awful lot to give as a player. It was such a shame and I felt very sorry for him. Mike Pejic suffered the same fate when he also quit the game through injury that year. I look at photos now and again of the celebrations we had on the open-top bus after winning the league and I see Pej and Brian on them. It reminds me they were part of that squad then, even though neither of them played a single minute. It must have been very difficult for them to enjoy that moment having not been able to contribute to it. I know how they would have felt because I was in a similar position when we played Barcelona in the Super Cup second leg.

I missed the match through injury – Andy Blair played instead of me – and I didn't really want to be involved with the celebrations. I kept well away from it. I could have had a tracksuit on and been part of it on the pitch, but it wasn't about me, it was about the players who won the game. They deserved to take all the adulation from the fans. I couldn't get too enthusiastic with the celebrations.

Our first serious challenge before the league matches started was against Tottenham Hotspur in the Charity Shield. I thought it would be nice to play in a Charity Shield at Wembley, especially because the last time I played at Wembley the game was a shocker, a 0-0 against Everton in that 1977 League Cup Final. The Tottenham match was a bit strange for different reasons as we drew again, this time 2-2, but there was no extra time or replay. So, I never did get to experience what winning at Wembley feels like! I only played 45 minutes as well because I had to come off, injured. I jumped for the ball and a Tottenham player put his knee in my back about half an hour into the game. I don't know who it was but by half-time I couldn't carry on. It was disappointing – that was my time at Wembley all done with. I would have loved more game time at Wembley, but it wasn't to be. Still, it was a great day out for the fans, with the trophy shared. It was a downer for me personally, but I knew we had bigger things to play for that season.

We started the campaign at Villa Park with a pre-match lap of honour, showing off our league championship trophy in front of our appreciative supporters and the newly promoted Notts County supporters. On paper it looked the perfect, low-key curtain-raiser for us to start with a victory, but it wasn't to be and they spoiled our party with a 1-0 win. It was a terrible start to the season for us actually and only a few games in, quite a few in the media had already written us off. We didn't exactly do ourselves justice, though, losing our first two games to County and then Sunderland – two clubs that only narrowly avoided relegation. It wasn't good enough for a reigning champion to be losing those types of games. Notts County went on to do the double over us.

One of the factors to our inconsistency was that we started to see more injuries, which I guess was inevitable – Gary Shaw, Gary Williams and Ken McNaught all missed games early on in that season and the rest of us didn't play as much either as in 1980/81. Shawsy was replaced by Terry Donovan and with all due respect, Terry wasn't Shawsy or at his level. He would have been better suited to replacing Withey. Des Bremner had to drop from midfield at times to play at the back; even Gary Williams was switched to centre-back at times. We had 24 players make a league appearance in that campaign, which was ten more than the season prior, which tells its own story. It tested us.

Ron Saunders was a big believer in the Liverpool philosophy. Something they always did every summer was bring in a big player or two, just to keep the players that were there on their toes and add squad depth. But at Villa, Ron was limited with what he had to spend. Our gates weren't always as big as you might think – there were just over 25,000 fans at Villa Park for the Stoke City match a month into the new season, which was an awfully low gate considering where we were as a club. I believe unemployment in Birmingham was a contributing factor, but all the same, that was the reality.

Our disappointing, inconsistent league form was constant through the season but fortunately we had the European Cup to provide a chink of light when there was gloom. A run of six consecutive league draws came either side of our first ever European Cup matches, with Icelandic side FC Valur. We treated the matches no differently to any other game as we started at home in front of only 20,000 fans. We never expected much from them as they were part-timers and it was good to put a score on the board, even without three of our first-choice players in Gary Shaw, Ken McNaught and Gary Williams, as we took a 5-0 lead to Reykjavik. The away match was just about finishing off the job, which we did courtesy of two goals from Shawsy, who returned from injury. It was like playing at an English non-league ground, in terms of the quality of the opposition and the basic surroundings.

The most striking thing for me about our visit to this ground was the nasty fish smell blowing across the pitch. Don't ask me why! Another thing I remember is the weird fashion sense they had locally. They all seemed to be wearing these big, thick woollen jumpers.

I brought a couple back actually but I'm not sure they went down very well with the recipients! It was fashion specially designed for their weather. It was so cold out there that Ivor Linton's afro hair almost froze solid through the wind-chill factor while he was sitting on the bench.

The following week we met up with an old friend, as Andy Gray returned to Villa Park with Wolves in the League Cup. He didn't exactly show me much love though when he took a whack at me and was sent off just after half-time. There was always plenty of banter between us on the pitch after he left Villa and there was no love lost between us. His sending off was just a result of two players who didn't like each other very much by now after what had been said around the time he left Villa. It was unnecessary from Andy, as I wasn't a player who ever set out to injure anyone. It wasn't in my make-up. But clearly feelings were still raw just two years after he had joined Wolves from Villa and he felt like he needed to hit out at that somebody and that somebody was me.

I don't have a great recollection of the incident, but I know he described it in his book as 'a hack'. I was quite adept at seeing when a rough challenge was coming and being able to avoid it. I liked nothing more than skipping over an intended kick and going on a run and seeing them still on the deck. I wasn't a dirty player and anyone that watched my career would know that. But I did lay out Trevor Brooking once. It was ironic that it was Trevor because he was a nice guy. But I inadvertently smashed him with my elbow straight on the nose while trying to intercept a ball on the halfway line. I felt nothing, carried on with an attack and the whistle blew. We were called back for a free kick and all these West Ham players surrounded me and said, 'What are you doing?' I had no idea what they were going on about. They said, 'Look at Trevor, you've laid him out!' It was news to me, as I felt nothing. I'm not proud of it as that wasn't how I played but it is kind of funny in hindsight.

We were soon back on the road in the European Cup, which started to come as a bit of a relief from our patchy league form. I'm positive, though, at the time we would all have been adamant we could climb the league.

The East Germans, Dynamo Berlin, were up next. It was a real eye-opener to go behind the Iron Curtain. I couldn't help but think to myself, 'What's gone wrong here? Why are they not living like we are? What's holding them back?' There was no wealth at all and the shops that I saw reminded me of Liverpool as a boy in the 1950s and 60s when we'd go to TJ Hughes just because it was cheap.

Everything seemed so colourless and monochrome. I had a walk around and everyone seemed to be dressed in black as though they were going to a funeral. East Berlin was eerily poor and a little spooky like something we had seen before in a Cold War spy film. We didn't do much sightseeing, but we visited the Berlin Wall and Checkpoint Charlie. I certainly wouldn't have been keen to go out on my own, especially for a drink, though

I don't doubt a few of the lads who couldn't sit still for five minutes would have ventured out and found a bar somewhere. And as became a bit of a recurring theme on our European journey – at least until we played Anderlecht – we stayed at another shit-hole of a hotel.

I played cards sometimes with the lads. There were two schools. The one that played for fun, which I was part of, and then the school that played for money. Drinking and gambling weren't my thing. So, what did I do to relax? I was different to most of the other lads as I was an avid reader, and while many of the lads would be happy playing cards either on the bus or at the hotels we stayed at, I would often read a book because that was the best way for me to relax and to avoid the monotony of the same routine, up and down a motorway.

I was into Alistair MacLean, who wrote thrillers, and Harold Robbins, who I was told wrote a lot about sex but when I read them I thought, 'Where's the sex?' They were just excellent stories. Desmond Bagley was another author whose books I loved to read. I loved to get into spy thrillers and adventures. I never used to be a good reader at home, but I found books helped me to relax before a game or on the bus when we were travelling. I wasn't a good sleeper either so reading in my room at night was another way that I was able to make myself tired, to get a good night's sleep. Peter Withe could sleep on a coffee table but I wasn't like that.

As far as the games went, they were hard encounters. Their lads were very strong and fit. I felt that with them being from behind the Iron Curtain and all that we learned about some East German and Russian athletes, it wouldn't be a surprise if a certain amount of trickery had gone on and they were on drugs, like steroids. I'm not accusing them, but it wouldn't surprise me because these blokes were proper physical specimens. It was a real battle. As regards the game, it will always be remembered, rightly, for Tony Morley's goal of the season when he ran the length of the pitch and for Jimmy's penalty save that helped keep us in it. The 2-1 win afforded us the luxury of losing 1-0 at home and going through on the away goals rule. They were the only goals we conceded in the whole campaign. The highlight of the round, on top of Tony's goal in Berlin, was just the level of resilience we showed to overcome their physicality.

Another two home defeats in the league either side of that second leg with Berlin showed yet again that we were really struggling to put a string of good results together. People have questioned whether we started to focus more on the European Cup at the expense of the league but it's a huge 'no' as far as I was concerned. I understand the question as we never made it into the top ten all season. However, I didn't think our European campaign was the sole target of our season as I wanted to win the league again or at least finish high enough to qualify for Europe. The time gaps between the different rounds were so spread out there was no way we could just have concentrated on the European Cup and then take our foot off the pedal for the league matches.

There were four months, for instance, between our match against Berlin and Dynamo Kyiv.

I always felt we had plenty of time to put things right in the league, but it just never happened. I can honestly say I never felt distracted. I can't speak for all the lads as some of them might have felt distracted by the European Cup and seeing this massive dream of the final at the end of the season. But I never did. My dream was winning the league again, like Liverpool often did. I wanted to stick two fingers up to all those who doubted us or those who said we were a one-season wonder but as far as our league form went that season, we simply weren't good enough. Therefore, the overriding story of 1981/82 was the European Cup. Our old rivals Ipswich were runners-up again and you have to admire their consistency, but they had lots of international experience in their squad to stand these ongoing challenges better than we did.

Farewell Ron, Hello Rotterdam

'The team was surprised Ron had left
so suddenly and most of us would have
been disappointed, but nobody would
have been gutted. We were focused on
our targets of winning league games and
in the European Cup. Some players are
affected by these things, but I never was.
I saw players and managers come and go
and it was part of the game'

WE ALL knew from what was being written in the press that Ron Saunders was having problems with the owner Mr Bendall, especially over his contract. Those issues were obvious. But what wasn't obvious is that Ron, given the resilient character he was, would throw the towel in.

The night before he walked out on Aston Villa, he phoned me. He said, 'Listen, I'm in a battle with the club, but you know me, I like battles, everything will be ok.' That was his way of giving me the truth from the horse's mouth in case any reporter called me to say otherwise or to get any quotes out of me on the situation. He was basically saying he wasn't going anywhere and would ride out the storm. So, for him to resign the very next day shows how difficult a situation he must have been put in because he certainly wasn't expecting to leave.

We had lost 4-1 at Manchester United on the Saturday that weekend, but Ron didn't act any differently after the match to any other game. That was typical Ron, though. He would be the same whether we had won comfortably or lost badly. He made that call to me the following evening. There was nothing out of the ordinary with that defeat at United other than the fact we lost again because we were missing three of our key players.

Once Ron left, I never saw him or spoke to him again for almost a year, until his Birmingham City side beat us on Boxing Day. I never even had his phone number at any time. The team was surprised he had left so suddenly and most of us would have been disappointed, but nobody would have been gutted. We were focused on our targets of winning league games and progressing in the European Cup. Some players are affected by these things, but I never was. I saw players and managers come and go and it was part of the game.

Maybe it sounds cold, but I *was* detached as a player. I believe it was a result of my upbringing at Coventry. I became friendly with players and then they'd leave. It could upset you that your best mate has gone. For instance, Ivan Crossley, who I joined Coventry with, stayed for a year and was gone not long after. It made me become more single-minded and not get too wrapped up in other people's business.

We were 15th in the league when Ron left in February 1982, yet we had qualified for the European Cup quarter-finals of course. We ended up improving our position in the table slightly to 11th under the new manager Tony Barton, but the league campaign must still go down as a huge disappointment. It ultimately comes down to the fact that our squad wasn't strong enough to cope with injuries; the kind of injuries we never suffered the previous season.

That's not an intentional slight against Dave Geddis, Terry Donovan, Andy Blair, Brendon Ormsby or anyone else. I certainly didn't think that at the time and would never have criticised anyone. But the results don't lie. A 4-1 loss at home to Leeds United towards the end of the season was a good example of how we struggled once we had a few regulars out. Myself, Shawsy and Evo missed that match and we lost heavily to a team which was relegated that season. It wasn't good enough for a club that was on the verge of winning the European Cup.

Further evidence came in the fact we came away with an honourable draw at Nottingham Forest three days before the Leeds game, but we had a full-strength team out that evening. And Cloughie would have wanted to have got one over on us then, knowing we were heading to the European Cup Final. No doubt the squad depth was one of the reasons why Ron became so frustrated with the board when they wouldn't give him the money to strengthen. When we were at our best and able to pick our best team, we were a match for anybody, as the final with Bayern Munich proved. But too often we either weren't at our best or at full strength.

It was a bonus for us that Tony Barton stayed on to replace Ron because he didn't change much. If Bendall had gone out and brought in a new face to manage Villa, things might have turned out very differently if that person had wanted to stamp their authority on the position. It helped that Ron and Tony were very similar characters in terms of being thoughtful with a quiet confidence and neither were shouters. They preferred to give you confidence by talking to you. I don't remember one confrontation during my Villa career with either Ron or Tony. So, the dressing room dynamic did not change all that much after Ron left.

Besides, the players in the team were also strong characters and we didn't allow Ron's departure to change anything. I have never known a single player lose sleep over a manager leaving his job. You might not like him leaving if you get along with that manager, as was the case with Ron, but players are more likely to be upset by one of their team-mates leaving if they are good mates with them. On the plus side, Ron leaving did have a positive impact on his number two Roy MacLaren, as he had to step up as the coach. He had been a bibs-and-cones-style coach as Ron was very hands-on at the training ground. But now he was leading training sessions in a way he had not done before.

Post-Ron, the next big challenge came in the shape of Dynamo Kyiv, though we were unable to play in Kyiv due to the freezing weather, so we headed a few hundred miles south to Simferopol in Crimea. If we thought East Berlin was bad, this was much worse.

Again, it was colourless as a place and the hotel was as bad as you could possibly imagine. The toilets in the rooms looked as if they had never been cleaned and most were without seats, there were no lids on the cisterns, while the beds looked like surplus military steel camp-beds. It was never going to be a comfortable stay. Even at the game there appeared to be more soldiers than supporters. We did well to come away with a goalless draw as they were good footballers and very strong. I reflect on these games sometimes and think, 'Wow, we had some serious resilience the way we came through these stern challenges.' We were much more comfortable in the second leg at Villa Park when goals from Ken and Shawsy put us through to the semi-finals.

I got injured in that home match against Kyiv, with only about two minutes to go. I played a one-two on the edge of their box and as I went for the return, one of their players tripped me up as I went past him. I fell awkwardly on my left arm. I didn't hear a crack, but I was sure I had broken it as I was in absolute agony. My elbow was facing the wrong way when I fell, and I think it was dislocated, with ligament damage. At the time I thought this might just be my season done and the end of my European dream.

It was the worst possible time to get injured because I needed to get away from the ground quickly and go to hospital for an X-ray.

The crowds of people streaming away from Villa Park made it almost impossible for a vehicle to move. I should have been put in an ambulance with the sirens blaring but Doc Targett, in his wisdom, put me in the back of his car and decided to drive me. Bad idea. I was sitting there in my kit – shorts, mud and all, stuck in traffic for over an hour for a journey that should have taken five minutes. They treated me and sent me home in a taxi as I couldn't drive. The news of no broken bones was obviously good, but I missed out on some great celebrations with the boys in the dressing room. To this day I still don't know how those celebrations went! Not that I needed beer or champagne in the dressing room, but the whole reason I played football was to have those moments, enjoying victory with your mates and especially in a huge tournament such as this.

At least I had the opportunity to enjoy the moment in Belgium after we overcame Anderlecht in the semi-finals.

We were keen to get our noses in front after being drawn at home for the first leg and thanks to another great goal from Tony Morley we were able to do that. The general feeling was that Anderlecht were quite a boring team and played very defensively. It was only after watching the final back that I realised both

Anderlecht and Bayern set up in a similar way, sitting back and guarding against our counter-attacks. It was quite clever of them because we did like to soak up pressure and when we went forward, we did so with pace and purpose, so they were wary of leaving themselves too open. This is why in those three games you only saw two goals, thankfully both scored by us.

The big talking point of the second leg in Brussels was the crowd disturbance after a guy ran on the pitch and laid down. I didn't see him at first. But the referee eventually had to stop the game and it became a real problem. I was later told that our fans were provoked – it never took much to get English fans going. Villa fans, though, were generally well behaved. I would question how the Anderlecht authorities allowed both sets of supporters to be situated so close to each other. It was a miscalculation by the club and the chaos it created made for an unsavoury stoppage to the game and the subsequent negative headlines.

When we reached the dressing room at the end of the game, it was just pure jubilation on making it through to the final. We were all celebrating and slapping each other on the back. The furthest thing from our minds at that stage was the possibility of an enquiry into the crowd trouble that might get us kicked out of the competition. We enjoyed the moment. Allan Evans said he enjoyed the feeling of qualifying for the final more than he enjoyed the final itself, as it was such a huge relief. I see where Evo is coming from there. I was usually quite pragmatic myself and that moment of reflection in the Anderlecht dressing room was another reminder to me of why I play football. I saw it as another opportunity to win a trophy as I had only been in one final by that stage.

News started to surface within a few days of the semi-final about politicians getting involved, discussing the issues of what to do. I don't think UEFA were that keen to throw us out of the competition – I felt it was sour grapes from Anderlecht. Fortunately, we were allowed to play the final and got away with a stadium ban for the first round the following season.

I get asked every now and again how I prepared for the European Cup Final in Rotterdam because there is no doubt it was the biggest game of my career. But the simple answer is I never did anything different. I was so focused on doing well once we got there that I did not want to get caught up in the excitement and hype surrounding it. I think that is more for families and friends, which is why I tried to keep my distance from people sometimes. All my family is in Merseyside anyway so had I played for Liverpool and reached a European final I'm sure the hype around me would have been overwhelming. But that wasn't the case for me as an Aston Villa player. It was probably for the best as it allowed me to stay relaxed and driven. I was at home with my wife and son and just enjoyed being a family man and new father.

We flew out to Rotterdam a couple of days early and stayed Monday and Tuesday night before the big match on the Wednesday. We didn't do much training in Holland as we had just finished a hard season and it was a matter of kicking a ball around, fine-tuning and staying fresh, nothing too intense. There were a lot of people around while we were training as well so we weren't keen to show the whole world what our free-kick routines were or anything like that. Any tactical discussions we had were done at the team hotel. I can't recall talking about Bayern Munich at all, though. That was never our style to worry about the opposition. We were very relaxed, there was no anxiety or intensity around the camp.

Some of the guys went out on the Tuesday afternoon for a few beers because they couldn't sit around for long. I was different. One thing football gave me, as well as a career, was patience. You do a lot of hanging around waiting for games and I liked to find ways to help me to relax and take my mind off football. As I've mentioned, I did a lot of reading. I would spend a whole afternoon reading a book. Something else I liked to do was listen to my Sony Walkman. I recorded my own mix tapes. Actually, just before we flew out to Rotterdam, Sony gave us all a Walkman so we had one each. So that was me – reading, listening to music, or maybe having a walk if there was anything to see. I didn't need anything else. One thing I do regret was not doing more photography in these interesting places I travelled to. I would have liked to keep a diary as well as I had the means to do it.

If I mixed with any of the lads it tended to be with Jimmy, Ken, Withey and Swainy. We might have played a game of cards, but I certainly wouldn't have had a drink on that Tuesday night. Not even a shandy. I had a good night's sleep and I was game-ready by Wednesday evening. We would have stayed in our rooms most of that day. Maybe a few would have ventured out for a game of cards. My music was enough to keep me relaxed, though.

Strangely, I have a patchy memory of the final and people have told me that's probably because I was in the zone. I can only recall certain things about the final with any detail. One was the performance of our rookie goalkeeper Nigel Spink, who obviously was brought on as sub after just nine minutes. I seldom praise keepers for making saves as that's why they're in the team. But the difference here was the situation and the fact Spinksy was only playing his second game for Villa. It took great character to play the game that he did. He deserved all the credit that came his way.

I never had a clue about Jimmy's injury. It was a complete shock to me when I saw him going off. It wasn't ideal but we never had time to dwell on it and we knew Spinksy was a good keeper because he trained with us every day. So, we had to get on with it as there was a game to be played. I didn't think it at the time but afterwards I did reflect, 'Wow, Nigel could have had a stinker and let the team down after being thrown in at the deep end like that. That could have ruined him before his career had barely begun.' But thank God he came off the pitch as the hero. It was probably the beginning of the end for Jimmy because everyone was able to see how good a keeper Nigel was. Halfway through the next season, Jimmy played his last game for us.

The other moments I recall with clarity are Tony's mazy run down the left to set up Withey for the goal, then me picking the trophy up. Everything else is a blur.

We couldn't play the game we wanted to for reasons I touched on before. We had to match them in the midfield battle, and it was like a chess match. Their extra international quality meant they had more chances but thankfully we, and especially Spinksy, were equal to them. They did their homework on us very well and stayed deep all through the game. We rarely got in behind them and the one time we did, with Tony's signature dribble down the left, it led to the goal.

Moments before I got my hands on the trophy, I thought, 'So this is what it's all about!' I'd watched Liverpool enjoy this moment so often and I wanted a piece of it, especially when I saw Forest win it twice also. This was my time now and I was so excited that I was going to be the one to get my hands on the European Cup first, before anyone else. Being captain isn't always a privilege but at that moment, it most certainly was.

I was so impatient about that moment that not long after the final whistle I walked over towards the steps where we had to go up to collect our medals and the trophy. The rest of the lads were celebrating with our fans behind the goal at one end of the ground – I wasn't. Not because I didn't want to, I was just like a kid at Christmas waiting to open my presents. I couldn't wait to get my hands on that European Cup. It took a while for the lads to join me. A UEFA official came over to me and said we need to get on with the presentation so can you please fetch your team-mates. I said, 'No, they're having fun. You go and get them, I'll wait here.'

Raising that trophy was a magical feeling. When I held it aloft, I felt like I didn't want to pass it over to anyone else. After having my time with it, I did eventually hand it over to the lads and probably didn't touch it again until we got back to our hotel in Amsterdam for the reception.

Several of the lads swapped shirts with Bayern Munich players like Tony, Des, Swainy, Lionel (Andy Blair) and Evo, but I was conscious of not doing that and had no intention of swapping my shirt. To be fair to Evo, he had it in his mind that he wanted to swap shirts with Karl-Heinz Rummenigge and he knew the best way to make that happen was while they were both on the pitch. There was no way, though, I was going to walk up those steps and lift the European Cup for Aston Villa while wearing a Bayern Munich shirt. It was never going to happen. It would have been the pits for me. I don't think I could have lived with that memory had I been wearing the red of Bayern. I asked Evo recently whether he regretted swapping his Villa shirt on that special night and he said he didn't. I told him if he was captain, he would think differently.

We had a few sherbets at our Amsterdam hotel – even me – but by the time we had celebrated in the dressing room after the match and then celebrated some more on the bus driving from Rotterdam to Amsterdam, where we met up with our families, we were shattered.

We were so keen to meet up with our families that we barely remembered to bring the European Cup off the bus. We put it in the toilet so that it would be safe and when we all disembarked to go to the hotel, only an afterthought by one of the lads meant we remembered to rescue it!

I met up with Jan at the hotel and the wives had endured a long day travelling as well, so they were ready for some sleep themselves. I don't know how late some of the younger lads stayed up or even if they went to bed at all, but I had about an hour in the bar and then hit the sack at about 1.30am. We had an early flight back into East Midlands Airport. Not ideal, but nobody was complaining!

With my brothers (from the left) Steve, Brian, Jeff and my Dad, Joe. This was taken at an early Coventry game, probably after we played Liverpool.

Here I am with my Kirkby Boys district team. Kenny Swain is back row, far right; Terry McDermott, front centre, and yours truly is front left.
Inset: David Johnson, me, Phil Thompson, Terry McDermott and Kenny Swain.

Alf Walton, the scout who spotted me and who took me to Coventry City as a 15-year-old. I have him to thank for my career.

My first professional contract as a pro footballer for £7 a week, rising to £10 in my third year. How times have changed!

10. In consideration of the observance by the said player of the terms, provisions and conditions of this Agreement, the said   A. J. LEATHER

on behalf of the Club hereby agrees that the said Club shall pay to the said Player the sum of £7. -. -.   per week from

September 1967   to   4th April 1968

and £8. -. -.   per week from   5th April 1968

to   4th April 1969   and £10. -. -.   per week from

5th April 1969   to   5th April 1970

11. This Agreement (subject to the Rules of The Football Association) shall cease and determine on   5th April 1970

unless the same shall have been previously determined in accordance with the provisions hereinbefore set forth.

Fill in any
other pro-
visions

As a Sky Blue,
making my way in
the game

Always a shame not to win when you reach a final but I enjoyed the battle with Graeme Souness, until he clobbered me and got sent off!

Tracking the fiery Leeds midfielder Billy Bremner. I reckon this was the match when he throttled me round my neck.

It was only a friendly but this letter and another one asking me to meet up for a gathering with other England hopefuls gave me hope of an England call-up.

DON REVIE ESQ.,
c/o The Football Association,
16 Lancaster Gate,
London,
W2 3LW.

Our ref: DR/jc   10th October, 1974

D. Mortimer Esq.,
Coventry City F.C.

Dear Sir,

Testimonial Match – Mr. Eric Taylor

The Football League Secretaries' and Managers' Association in conjunction with Sheffield Wednesday Football Club has arranged for a Testimonial match for the late Mr. Eric Taylor, to be played at Hillsborough on Monday, 21st October, 1974, and I have been asked to select and manage an All Star XI to play against Sheffield Wednesday Football Club on this occasion.

I am enclosing a list of a squad of 15 players whom I have selected, and I do hope that you will be able to accept my invitation to play in this match. I have, already, obtained the approval of your Club's manager for you to take part.

You are asked to report to the Royal Victoria Hotel, Victoria Station Road, Sheffield (telephone number: Sheffield 78822), by 4.30p.m. on the day of the match. Overnight accommodation will be arranged for you at the Hotel if you require it for the Monday night, but if you wish to return to your home immediately after the match you will be free to do so.

Will you kindly complete the attached acknowledgement sheet, and return it to me at the above address as soon as possible, confirming that you will be available to play in the match, and also letting me know whether you require Hotel accommodation for the night of Monday, 21st October.

Yours faithfully

Don Revie
Team Manager

Enc.

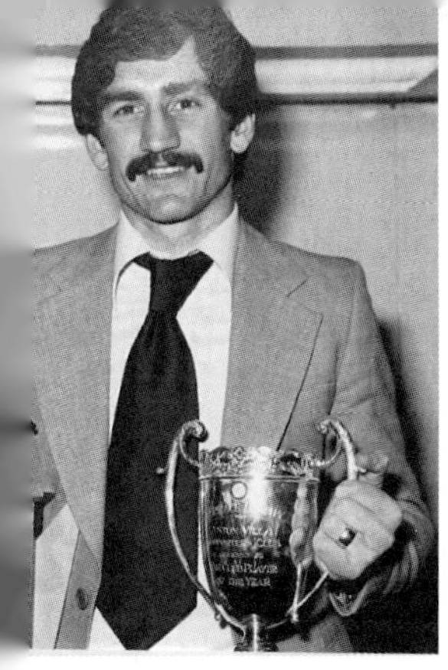

After a slow start at Villa, it was satisfying to win this Supporters' Player of the Year Award to finally prove myself to the fans.

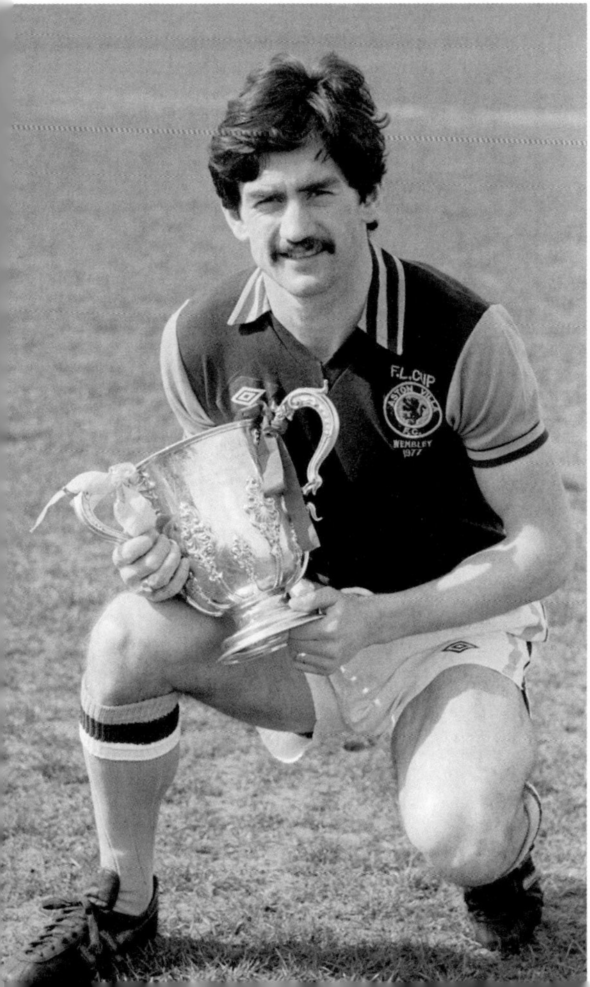

Holding the League Cup that we won in 1977. It was one trophy but could easily have been three.

Me, John Burridge, Chris Nicholl and Andy Gray looking very happy after beating Everton in the 1977 League Cup Final.

It wasn't easy to get close to the great Johan Cruyff but was great just to play against the Dutch master, in our 1978 UEFA Cup quarter-final.

In the dressing room and enjoying the moment at Highbury after winning the league championship, despite a 2-0 defeat that day.

Ron Saunders wasn't seen smiling in front of the cameras very often but he had good reason to here after winning the league.

It was always a pleasure to wear
the claret and blue of Aston Villa,
which has been my adopted
team despite growing up a
Scouser.

Picking up the award for my Goal
of the Season against Stoke City
in 1979/80. Bryan Robson (right)
was still a West Brom player then.

Nigel Spink, Des Bremner, Frankenstein, Kenny Swain and me, at Universal Studios in Los Angeles on our post-season trip in the summer of 1981. I'd rather have gone to Spain!

Not the Wembley memory I wanted, going off injured and only sharing the Charity Shield with Spurs but here I am, with their skipper Steve Perryman.

Parading the league
championship trophy
with the Villa fans at the
first home game of the
1981/82 season. Shame
we lost that day!

What a night! Celebrating our European Cup with manager Tony Barton and match-winner Peter Withe, who never scored a more important goal in his career.

I never got tired of holding that trophy up in Rotterdam and I probably irked my team-mates by holding on to it too long!

Shaking hands with my opposition captain and Italy legend Dino Zoff when we played Juventus in the European Cup in 1982/83. They were just too strong for us over both legs.

Lining up against my old mate Andy Gray after he signed for Wolves. It's sad that our relationship deteriorated in more recent years.

I was glad to get away from Villa Park in the end after being frozen out by Graham Turner. I enjoyed my season by the sea at Brighton, shame it wasn't for longer.

It was not my plan to play for Villa's bitter rivals, Birmingham City, but I was a professional and had to play where I was wanted. And John Bond wanted me.

On the bench…as assistant manager to Keith Burkinshaw at West Bromwich Albion

Posing with the great Brazilian footballer Rivellino on a Copa Pele veterans' tour of Brazil in 1989. Great fun. The other photo is one I took of ex-Everton player Alan Whittle with famous train robber Ronnie Biggs.

Never too late to have a degree, thanks here to Worcester University.

Catching up with Peter Withe, Ken McNaught, Tony Morley, Des Bremner and Gordon Cowans, at the Wembley play-off final between Villa and Fulham in 2018. Apparently my co-author Richard Sydenham was somewhere behind the goal!

What an honour, to have Michel Platini present us with a memorial plaque, marking the small part that we played in the European Cup's then 60-year history.

It's always fantastic when all the lads from 1982 get back together to reminisce. Our AV40 anniversary tour allowed us to spend plenty of time together. Here we are at Villa Park.

On Borrowed Time as Deadly Returns

'I was devastated. As soon as he came
back to the club, I just knew what was
going to happen. I had this feeling that he
would try to break our team up'

THE 1982/83 season should have been a great campaign for Aston Villa. Rotterdam was now a memory, but its legacy was that we would be challenging for six competitions.

To only claim one of them and fail to even get close in four of them was disappointing. We had the usual domestic competitions ahead of us – the league, the FA Cup, the League Cup; and there was also the European Cup to defend, the World Club Championship and the European Super Cup.

We let ourselves down for the most part but there was one major event that transpired in the winter of 1982 that had a major impact on Aston Villa. I would say it was a major catastrophe when 'Deadly' Doug Ellis bought the club off the Bendalls and, unlike the last time he was at Villa, there was nobody to stop his one-man dictatorship.

Before that situation came about, I have to say our manager Tony Barton didn't make the best of starts in his first full season as Villa boss. The one thing he should have done was keep our well-drilled, disciplined first team intact and add a few quality players to strengthen the squad. But he seemed to panic when we lost our first two league games when he dropped Kenny Swain.

That was strange. Admittedly it was a dreadful start, losing 3-1 at home to Sunderland and then 5-0 at Everton. Those results were not just down to Kenny, but Tony seemed to hold him responsible and made him his first real change post-Rotterdam. That was Tony's first big mistake. There was not much going on in the top echelons of English football that Brian Clough wasn't aware of and he acted swiftly on hearing of Kenny's development. Kenny moved to Nottingham Forest, on loan initially and then permanently, and kept an England international out of the team in Viv Anderson.

Kenny had so much more to offer and, by all accounts, he was one of the star players for the next two seasons at Forest. I felt it was a poor and costly decision by Tony to move him on so soon after the highs of Rotterdam and our European Cup campaign, especially given all of the competitions we were in that season. Mark Jones came in initially at right-back and would play 17 league matches that season. He was a decent player coming through from the youth team, but he was nowhere near ready to replace an experienced player like Swainy. If Kenny did start that season slowly – and he wouldn't have been the only one, I can tell you – I know he would have put things right. I'm very critical of the role Doug Ellis played in several players' subsequent departures, but Swainy's was totally on Tony Barton.

While Villa had to find a new right-back, I lost my regular room-mate. But as one door closes..! I started rooming with Mark Walters thereafter and I enjoyed being a kind of mentor figure with him as he was always a good lad and was a special player. He made things happen out of nothing with a spark of magic. I knew, as with Gary Shaw, that if he kept his head right and his feet on the ground, he would become a great player.

We made light of our first European Cup defence by overcoming Turkish outfit Besiktas, including a 3-1 behind-closed-doors win at home, our punishment for the Anderlecht away leg. It was like playing a practice match at Bodymoor Heath.

Dinamo Bucharest were up next and those games were all about Gary Shaw. He notched both of our goals away from home, then fired in a hat-trick at Villa Park as we won those games 2-0 and 4-2 respectively. Shawsy must have been buzzing as he ended up with 24 goals that season.

He had a starter season in 1979/80, linked up with Peter in 1980/81, which was the best thing since sliced bread for him. Then in 1981/82 he became a European

Cup winner. Now he was entering his third full season and finished it as our top scorer. There must have been so much going on in his exciting, young life. He was showing that he had all the capabilities to become a great England player because, as I've said, he was in the same mould as Kenny Dalglish.

His career was looking so rosy and you couldn't see anything else other than him going on to earn many caps for England and being a prolific goalscorer for Villa, which, of course, was his boyhood club. Peter and Gary brought each other into the game but the great thing about Gary was that he brought us – the midfield – into the game too and linked up perfectly. For me, Gary was the blue-eyed boy of football then. Every reporter wanted a piece of him and it wasn't difficult to understand why.

We were up to third in the league by the start of December, after a run of five wins in six games, but any positivity or optimism flying around then was soon shot down by the news of Ellis's return.

I was devastated. As soon as he came back to the club, I just knew what was going to happen. I had this feeling that he would try to break our team up. I was so disappointed that the consortium led by Harry Parkes, a former Villa player and then a local businessman, had not won their bid to buy the club. I'm certain that if Harry had owned Villa, the club would have gone on to greater glories. I don't think Harry and his associates would have been more concerned with any existing debt than having a good team. Once Ellis was in charge he was only concerned about money and cutting costs. Never the players. Ellis was obsessed by the debt that he, apparently, inherited on his return to the club.

Previously when Doug had been around, we had Ron Saunders to control the board and, indirectly, Ellis. He had a strong influence when dealing with directors and his success at Villa had earned that level of authority. Ron was gone now, though, and there was nobody to challenge Ellis. Aston Villa was about to become a very unhealthy dictatorship and there were no other directors who had enough shares to be able to stand up to Ellis.

Ellis only ever wanted himself to be the centre of attention, not the team. It was all about him. He was prepared to run a mediocre football team that operated with far less expenditure than it had done. Eventually that plan backfired on him with a relegation, but that was after my time. But not long after!

The team was powerless to prevent what was going on off the field, of course. All we could do was try to keep our good run going. But, subconsciously, the Ellis takeover seemed to bring a black cloud over our season. We never fell out of the top ten all season but an end-of-season league finish of sixth could have been better.

Our first major challenge under the Ellis regime was a trip to Japan to play South American champions Penarol of Uruguay. No British team had ever won the World Club Championship and it felt like a great opportunity to go out there and change history. We didn't know much about them other than they were quite skilful and liked to pass the ball about. The game itself was a massive anti-climax, losing 2-0, and it reminded me of the Wembley League Cup Final against Everton in 1977. It was a real disappointment. It should have been a showcase game, and while it had the razzmatazz of Tokyo, I just feel we were short-changed. We played on a pitch that barely had any grass on it and with a lighter ball that we had never seen before. I'm not sure why we didn't practise with the same match ball, which you normally would, but we never did and the ball we played with was alien to what we were used to. It was like kicking a beach ball on the sand at Southport! These aren't excuses, they're just my memories of that game.

I had been to Japan before with Coventry. I found it an amazing, special place, a bit like New York. All these high-rise buildings with loads of flashing images on them all the time. It was like one big cinema. As energised as I was by the ambience of Tokyo, I wasn't into Japanese food so a few of us found ourselves looking for restaurants where I could get steak and chips, the philistines that we were! You were never going to find me in a sushi bar. I did, though, appreciate the buzz of the city and I wish I had taken my camera with me to capture some memories on film for posterity, but by that stage, I wasn't doing as much photography and had stopped developing my own black and white photos.

I was told by someone that on the plane home from Japan, Doug was looking at the cheque made out to the club with quite a bit of glee. He kept eyeing it up and couldn't take his eyes off it. He was less impressed, apparently, when it was pointed out to him that half of it was to be shared amongst the players as a bonus for winning the European Cup the previous season.

I'm not sure if it was delayed jet lag or the fallout from Japan, but we struggled to regain our form when we got back. We lost five of six games around that time and unfortunately that run of results led to the end of Jimmy Rimmer's Villa career. He was the next big casualty of the post-Rotterdam era after Kenny. A 4-2 loss at home to Liverpool and then a 3-0 defeat at Ron Saunders' Birmingham City over the Christmas period did for Jimmy. He was permanently dropped for the younger Nigel Spink, who had obviously proven himself on a global scale in the European Cup Final months earlier.

To be fair to Jimmy, these were probably two games he could have done without after a long-haul flight. He had been outstanding for us for five seasons hardly missing a game. Yes, he had a bit of a blip here and there, but what goalkeeper never has a blip? It's clear to me the ousting of Jimmy wasn't just about football. This was Doug Ellis's first proper axing of a league championship and European Cup winner. Jimmy was the highest-paid player in our team, so it wasn't a hard decision for Ellis to push him out. I have no doubt he would have put Tony Barton under pressure to leave Jimmy out of the team.

Ousting Jimmy would certainly have been about money. Doug was always moaning that the club was in debt, over a million pounds apparently. He would then have started to think, 'Ok, let's start trimming the wage bill.' And Jimmy was the biggest target. His replacement, Spinksy, would probably have been on a third of Jimmy's money. This was typical of the way Ellis thought. His mentality was more centred on, 'How can we cut costs?' than 'How can we build on our recent success?'

With all that said, I can understand why Tony would have wanted to introduce Nigel into the first team after his incredible baptism in Rotterdam. Jimmy was becoming an aged goalkeeper and Nigel had waited for his chance and was ready for his opportunity. To be fair to Tony, even after Rotterdam, he still kept faith in Jimmy and it was only after Ellis came back that he dropped him. Nigel, though, was a safe pair of hands. He was now our No.1 for the upcoming challenges, starting with Barcelona in the Super Cup.

It was my second visit to the Camp Nou after playing there in the UEFA Cup five years earlier. These are the games where you want to test yourself against the best, abroad. The one thing I took away from these games more than anything was how adept they were at committing what you might call professional fouls. They acted and pretended you kicked them, which was not something we saw much of in the English league, a more honest game.

They were two brutal Super Cup ties and we had to match them to come out on top, which we did, 3-0 on aggregate. That wasn't how we played the game, but I am quite proud that we proved we could mix it with them when required as well as play our football. I didn't play in the second leg, a 3-0 win at Villa Park, as I was injured with an Achilles problem. That game hinged on one moment, when Peter Withe smacked their centre-half with his elbow to set up our first goal. It just unsettled them. I don't especially like the fact we needed to elbow one of their players to change the course of the match, but Peter was an experienced centre-forward and he knew he had to do something to upset them. They were fouling us all night.

I picked up a medal, but I never joined in with the celebrations as I kept my suit on having not played any part in the match. It wasn't my style to want to be centre stage when I hadn't played in the game that clinched the trophy. I was happy to let stand-in captain Ken McNaught enjoy the moment as skipper on the night. I said we clinched 'the trophy', but it was just a wooden plaque!

The big nights at Villa Park were not done with the Barcelona win, as we welcomed Italian giants Juventus in the European Cup quarter-final in the March. It was like playing the World Cup-winning Italy side of 1982, plus Boniek and Michel Platini. There would have been a few thoughts of 'bloody hell, these guys are serious names we're taking on here' as was the case when we played Barcelona and Cruyff in 1978. But having been brought up on Ron Saunders' team talks, we wouldn't have been overawed or intimidated.

The main thing that cost us in that 2-1 first-leg defeat at Villa Park was the absence of Allan Evans. He was out and Des Bremner dropped back to take his place with Andy Blair coming into the midfield. Juve scored after 57 seconds courtesy of a Paolo Rossi header at the near post. I feel if Allan had been in the team, that goal wouldn't have happened. It was the worst possible start and Des was too slow in allowing Rossi to get ahead of him and aim his header into the net. If Evo and Big Ken were playing together, one of them would have made sure they got to the ball first. It wasn't Des's fault as he was not a central defender and we missed his legs and tackling in the midfield, but I guess it again showed our lack of depth in the squad.

We performed credibly enough against a team that was expected to win the competition that season, with eight of the 1982 World Cup winners in their team. Kyiv and Berlin were tougher teams to play physically, but Juventus had all the trickery and technique and were well ahead of most teams we had ever faced. We lost 3-1 in Turin on a miserable, wet night but we were far from shamed. I watched the game back on YouTube quite recently and Withey had a few far-post headed chances that he would normally have put away. There were other opportunities as well. It wasn't to be but it was no disgrace going out to this Juventus team.

It was a decent season, finishing sixth and qualifying for the UEFA Cup, but I can't help thinking 'what if?' on so many levels. What if we had won those last three league games that we lost, to clubs we should have been beating: Luton, West Ham and Swansea? Runners-up sounds better than sixth! What if we had beaten Penarol? What if Swainy hadn't been sold? We also lost another FA Cup quarter-final at Arsenal in between the two Juventus games. Again, what if?!

Over the 1983 summer, Tony replaced me as captain with Allan. I didn't know it at the time but I was soon to discover why. That summer was very nearly my last as an Aston Villa player. Tony met with the chairman and it was clear he had been advised to get rid of me, which didn't surprise me because I knew Ellis would want to offload a few more European Cup winners and build a team that he could say he was responsible for. It was all about Ellis making the big decisions now. We had already seen Kenny Swain leave, Jimmy was allowed to join Swansea that summer, and now Ken McNaught and Tony Morley soon followed them out of the club to West Brom. I was supposed to join Ken there, before Morley arrived.

Slowly, the manager was starting to change the team around, under instruction from Ellis in my view. Tony's first signing, in the March of 1983, was Alan Curbishley. That surprised me because I thought he was a similar player to Andy Blair. I didn't feel we needed to top up the squad numbers for the sake of it. Then, in the summer, goalkeeper Mervyn Day, centre-half Steve Foster, young striker Paul Rideout and the highly regarded Everton midfielder Steve McMahon all came in. McMahon was Tony's first *big* signing. I looked at Macca coming in and thought, 'He plays where I play.

What's going on here?' At that point Tony had not told me anything, or words to the effect that he was bringing McMahon in and I was being put up for transfer.

It wasn't until pre-season training when the squads started getting split up into groups that things became clearer. Tony picked his first team squad – and I was not in the picture. I was in the reserves for the inter-squad friendlies. It was the first time I realised that I was now surplus to requirements.

Not much was communicated to me about where my future lay. I don't ever recall Tony Barton telling me he didn't want me. It took a surprise phone call from Ron Wylie, the manager at West Bromwich Albion, to really bring it home that I needed to find another club. He told me he wanted to bring me over to West Brom. I said, 'Look Ron, it does seem that my opportunities are going to be less at Villa since the arrival of McMahon, but I still have another year left on my contract, so I'm in no rush to decide my future, though I don't want to be playing in the reserves either. I'll go on the pre-season tour with Villa and when I get back, I'll come over and have a chat with you.' That's how we left it. It was obvious Ron had been tipped off by Doug Ellis that I was available, as the two were very close friends.

The exodus from our Rotterdam team was well and truly under way. However, just when it seemed like I would be heading across the West Midlands to the Albion, something happened in Spain that indirectly extended my Aston Villa career for another two years.

Gordon Cowans suffered a badly broken leg and Tony Barton told me he couldn't let me leave now as it looked likely Gordon would be out of action for a long time. Tony knew he couldn't afford to lose the experience of Sid and me as he had spent his transfer budget already. I could have said 'no, I still want to go' out of principle at how I had been treated but I didn't. I never held anything against Tony because I knew it was Ellis who was really pulling the strings behind the scenes. I thought Tony was on my side and I knew it was Ellis who wanted me out. Tony was under pressure from Doug from day one.

The one positive to come out of this situation was that I saw the opportunity to negotiate with the club to try to improve my situation. I told Tony that if I stayed, I'd like another year on my contract plus a testimonial as it would be ten years at Villa in 1985. He said he would speak to the chairman. He eventually came back and said he had got me the extension of another year, but the chairman won't grant the testimonial.

I didn't want to leave Villa but with the way things were looking for me then, I might well have been better off financially to have moved to West Brom. They might have offered me a two- or three-year contract on decent money and with a signing-on fee. It's funny how things turn out, though. Having spent parts of the 1983 summer under the impression I was off to the Baggies, a year later I was being awarded the Fans' Player of the Year award at Villa. I played some of my best football in a long time.

It wasn't a great season in terms of the league finish again though (tenth). The way we exited the UEFA Cup was another blow. We had a credible 2-2 draw away at Spartak Moscow but threw it away at Villa Park. It was 1-1 with a minute to go and we went to sleep and allowed them to take a quick free kick and score a scruffy goal. We were out, after doing ever so well to keep a good side at bay. We hadn't learned our lesson from the first leg when we were winning 2-1 and conceded a last-minute equaliser. It's a skill to close out a game whether you're trying to win or draw. But we couldn't manage it in either leg.

One bright spark of the 1983/84 season was the League Cup. We had a wonderful opportunity to go back to Wembley but fell at the semi-final stage to Everton. I was dreaming of playing Liverpool in the final and enjoying the kind of spectacle at Wembley that we never had in 1977.

We lost 2-0 at their place in the first leg. It still annoys me when I reflect that I had the chance to poke the ball out for a corner for their first goal. I saw Spinksy out the corner of my eye and thought he had it covered. Unfortunately, he didn't and we both left it and the ball ended up going in as an Adrian Heath goal. It was a soft goal for us to concede and I could have prevented it.

The second goal was another poor one as we failed to clear the danger and allowed Kevin Richardson the chance to prod the ball home. To rub salt into our wounds, Richardson famously handballed on the line.

I don't know how the referee and the linesmen missed it as it was so blatant. That would have been 2-1 and while it wouldn't have meant we would definitely have gone to the final, the second leg at Villa Park would have been a totally different proposition with only one goal in it. But it wasn't to be.

A cup final would possibly have saved Tony Barton's job at the end of that season – at least if we had won it, anyway. But in the event, he was to become Deadly's first managerial sacking since his return to Villa Park and we would soon be meeting our next manager!

An Ignominious End

*'No Villa fan in their wildest dreams could
have imagined Graham Turner would
be the manager brought in to lead Villa
into the new season. I'm positive all Villa
supporters would have thought, "Graham
who?" I certainly thought that. He was an
anonymous name to me'*

NOBODY EXPECTED our new manager to have
the lack of pedigree that Graham Turner had, after he
was installed as the new Aston Villa manager in the
summer of 1984.

He had only ever played and managed in the
lower divisions so you have to say it was a shocking
appointment by the chairman. Most people would
think at least ten good managers would be prepared
to walk over broken glass to become the new boss of a
club like Aston Villa, two years after being champions
of Europe. To bring in the 36-year-old player-manager
from Shrewsbury Town was a desperation appointment

after so many good names backed away from the job, or – more to the point – refused to work for Doug Ellis.

No Villa fan in their wildest dreams could have imagined Graham Turner would be the manager brought in to lead the club into the new season. I'm positive all Villa supporters would have thought, 'Graham who?' I certainly thought that. He was an anonymous name to me. We had no idea of his philosophy on the game, how he wanted to play, and I wonder if he even knew himself what the top level was all about as he hadn't been anywhere near it as a player or manager. I'm not saying you always have to be a top player to make a good manager, but his lack of pedigree in elite football concerned a few of us. I hoped that if Ellis really didn't believe that Tony Barton was the right man to take us forward, he would then bring in an icon of the game who would be strong enough to stand up to him and retain the players he thought could still do a job for Villa. Sadly, that never happened.

If it had been Graham Taylor, now that would have been something after what he had done with Watford, taking them from the Fourth Division to the runners-up spot in the top tier, behind Liverpool in 1983. We need to ask why these guys who were linked with the vacant manager's job, or approached or even interviewed, walked away from Villa? Ok, some of them like Ron Atkinson and Keith Burkinshaw, who were apparently sounded out, were already employed at big clubs. But others were either unemployed or were at clubs that you would think they would be happy to walk out on, like John Toshack (Swansea City) and David Pleat (Luton Town).

It was obvious they stayed away from the role because they knew they would not have the autonomy to run the team the way they wanted. That was the way football managers operated in those days at the bigger clubs. They wanted to be in charge of everything, at least connected to the football team and transfers. But with Doug Ellis and maybe one or two other chairmen, what we started to see was businessmen who wanted more control of everything at their club.

We were therefore left with Graham Turner. You can't blame Graham for taking the job as it was a huge opportunity for him at that stage of his career, but even he would admit that job was way too big for him at that time. I believe Ellis looked at Turner as someone who he knew he could control and manage. I know Turner has denied that in the past, but I am sure he would have been put under pressure from the chairman to buy and sell certain players.

Over the years, reading various books and watching interviews with Ellis, he always gave me the impression that he thought he was an expert when it came to judging footballers. If that were true, why did he let so many of us leave when we all had at least two or three years left in us at Villa? The combination of us senior players and the talented lads coming through like Mark Walters, Tony Dorigo, Tony Daley and Paul Birch would have been a great set of players for any manager to inherit. Too many decisions that Ellis made were based around cost-cutting and Turner would undoubtedly have been a cheaper option than many of the more experienced managers who were associated with taking the job.

We all had to accept the decision and move on, but what it meant now more than ever was that we were all under scrutiny.

When Tony Barton took over from Ron Saunders, he knew us and subsequently didn't change much because he knew what we were all about. He scouted most of the lads anyway. But with Turner coming in, it was always likely he would change things to put his own stamp on the squad. And that is exactly what he did.

Turner's last away game as the Shrews' manager was at Cambridge United. His first away games for Villa were on a pre-season tour in Spain against Bayern Munich and Boca Juniors! Welcome to life at Aston Villa, Graham. They were close matches and there wasn't much in them (2-1 and 2-0) but the whole point of pre-season anyway is to improve your fitness and match sharpness ready for when the important games start in the league.

Turner clearly wanted to lay down a marker as this new, young manager and in the dressing room after the second of those defeats he told everyone that we couldn't go out for a beer. This was pre-season, remember, and some of the lads loved to go out and about and frequent the odd hostelry. I wasn't a boozer, so it didn't really affect me, but I didn't like how Turner tried to lay down the law so early in his tenure over something quite petty in the greater scheme of things. I wanted to stand up for the team and have a word with the manager. I thought, 'We haven't been hammered out here and we're going home tomorrow, let them have a drink.' But, of course, I wasn't the captain anymore, that was Allan Evans, so I stayed out of it.

When we got onto the training pitch, the status quo was soon to change. I read Turner's comments about me in *Ticket to the Moon*, when he basically said I made his job difficult in the early days of his tenure because I was a 'strong character'. I thought, 'What a load of bollocks.' The unfortunate thing is me and Des could have been his best players if he hadn't been so insecure and intimidated by us as senior players in the dressing room. Turner did talk up Peter Withe and Allan Evans and what good blokes they were in the dressing room, which they were. But me and Des were also good team men.

He came in with a preconceived plan, no doubt filtered down to him by the chairman. I think he sat down with Ellis and heard too much about what Ellis wanted to happen and he was keen to please his new chairman. If he had instead put his arm around me and Des and said, 'Look, I'm a new, young manager and I really want to tap into your experience and know-how about this club and the players,' we could all have benefitted each other so much. But he didn't go in that direction, which is sad. The ironic part of those comments from Turner is that Withey and Evo were more outspoken than me and Des. They would have made more of a noise than we did. Des and I just got on with our jobs.

Turner never once sat down with me as an individual to find out what I thought about the game or how I wanted to play. The first thing he should have done was call myself, Des, Peter and Allan into a room to sit down and discuss what this club was all about. He could easily have won us all over in one simple gesture like that – but he never because he was too insecure and feared our reputations as senior players. The four of us were miles ahead of where Turner was then in terms of what we knew about football in the top division and he should have embraced us, but he didn't.

He came to Villa without his own coach and eventually hired Malcolm Beard, but Malcolm had been working as a scout and had Tony Barton's old job. Subsequently, Turner took every training session, which was a big mistake. The impression I had was the only person he ever sat down with was Doug Ellis, to listen to what he wanted. There was no way Des and myself would have made trouble for him, we were seasoned professionals, but the more time went on, the more I came to the conclusion that he was listening to the chairman too much.

The 5-0 defeat at Villa Park against Nottingham Forest on Wednesday, 5 September 1984 was the first time in my career that I had ever been substituted without an injury, including my days as a rookie at Coventry. I couldn't believe it when I looked up and saw my number, which was now 11 by the way as Steve

McMahon had claimed my iconic No. 6 shirt. I didn't feel like I was playing under any pressure as we had won our first two games of the season with me and Des in the side and things were looking up. Then we lost 3-0 to Newcastle, when I had the displeasure of playing against the magical Peter Beardsley and Chris Waddle, but the Forest game was the one when things started to change.

I only played two more games for Aston Villa after this one. I don't understand how I ever got taken off because the player who was to blame for that result was Colin Gibson, and Gibbo himself would probably admit he didn't have his best game that night. It was only 1-0 on the hour mark after a speculative Ian Bowyer shot had somehow crept in, in the first half. Then in the second half, Gibbo allowed Steve Wigley to get past him and put a cross in three times and they scored on every occasion. Trevor Christie scored a hat-trick in less than half an hour! I was taken off at 4-0 down for Paul Rideout. I was bitterly disappointed. I felt that the midfield was doing its job. Myself, Des, Steve and Gordon Cowans were not getting overrun, the goals were all very soft and preventable.

The morning after that game at the training ground, Turner sat us down and said there would be a few changes in the team for the next game but never explained what they would be. We were soon to discover that it would be myself and Des who were being excluded in an effort to move us out of the club. I could have told the manager to sod off and refuse to train with the reserves but that wasn't in my make-up. I bit my lip, kept my head down and joined the reserves at Bodymoor Heath and trained under Bill Shorthouse.

Again, I feel Turner handled that situation badly. He could have sat down with the team and had an open and frank conversation about why we lost that match 5-0. He never once spoke to me or Des.

I found out that Turner never actually spoke to anyone about his plans when most managers have a confidante. I bumped into my old mate Brian Little at the training ground one day as Brian was coaching the youth team. I asked him, 'Does Turner speak with you about things and how he wants the youth team to play?' Brian said, 'No, we never talk. He comes in, gets changed, sits in his office, then he goes out on the training ground. That's it.' Brian left soon after that because he couldn't get along with Turner and he also didn't like the way his old mates, like me, were being treated.

Turner needed someone, like a number two, who could try to make him understand that there was more to the club than he was giving it credit for and more to the players who were already there.

I had no bitterness whatsoever towards Steve McMahon, who had taken my place – my issue was with the manager and especially the chairman. There is no doubt McMahon was a good, competitive player, though he could be reckless with his tackling at times when he didn't need to be. He was a better player than that and he proved it when he went to Liverpool. The talk amongst the lads, though, was always 'When is Macca going to get his move to Liverpool?' We were all aware of his desperation to get to Anfield from interviews we'd read in the media. It didn't seem a big secret, so Villa felt like a stepping-stone for him. Tony Barton would have been naïve if he ever thought McMahon came to Villa for the long term.

That said, McMahon and myself should have played a lot more together for the reason that Sid wasn't ready to play the number of games (34) that he did in the 1984/85 campaign. Sid never played a single game in the previous season because of that terrible leg break and injuries like that take a lot of coming back from. I played alongside Gordon for almost ten years and I knew when he wasn't at his best and this particular season he wasn't at his usual outstanding levels. He should have had a month or two in the reserves first, getting his match sharpness up. Turner subsequently sold Gordon to Bari in the summer of 1985 but in my view, he was making a judgement on a player who hadn't played at his best that season. I knew there was more to come, as we saw when he returned for two more relatively successful spells at Villa in later years.

While Des had got on the phone to Ron Saunders and managed to get himself a transfer to the Blues, my routine was training with the Villa reserves. Steve Foster had joined me by now after he also fell out of favour with Turner.

Since the Forest game, the first team beat Chelsea, drew at Watford, lost at home to Tottenham, then scraped a win over Scunthorpe in the League Cup, when McMahon got injured. With McMahon out, all the reserve lads kept saying to me, 'When's the gaffer going to call you over, because Macca is never going to be fit for [the next match at] Ipswich.' Turner would have been desperate for McMahon to recover so he didn't have to give me a recall. By the Friday, the day before the match, the reserves were already training at Bodymoor as McMahon came out of the changing rooms, late, to take his fitness test in a five-a-side with the first team. After five minutes, we could see he wasn't fit and went back inside.

While all this was going on, Fozzy was in my ear saying, 'He's got to call you over now!' Sure enough, Turner started to walk towards our pitch. Bill Shorthouse stopped our session and walked towards Turner. They met halfway, had a chat and Bill walked back to me and said, 'He wants you over there.' What was I to do? I could have done two things. I could have told Bill to let the manager know I'm not interested. Or I could be professional, not hold a grudge and get on with it. I chose the latter. Turner was still standing in the middle of the pitch, waiting for my response, and as I started to walk over towards him, he said: 'You can tell me to fuck off if you want.' He knew he'd treated me rotten. I said nothing and just kept walking. There was no need for me to respond, but I took some satisfaction from his acknowledgement that he had treated me badly. The way he dealt with me was terrible and no way to treat a player who had given so much to the club.

So, I was back in the team – and it was a forgettable comeback. I played my first game for Turner after spending almost a month with the reserves and we lost 3-0 at Portman Road. It never helped that both Gibbo and Withey were sent off with more than half an hour to go. It was only 1-0 when we still had all our players on the pitch. Our poor form saw us drop to 14th in the league table. I knew things had to change.

On the Monday morning after that Ipswich game, I thought it was the right time to have a chat with the manager. I knew once McMahon was fit again, I would be dropped and I wasn't happy about being a bit-part player. I felt I had an advantage after what he had said to me on the training pitch – it was the first time Turner had acknowledged treating me badly.

I said, 'Look, I've helped you out here. I haven't kicked up a fuss or rubbished you in the press,' which I could have done easily. I tried to appeal to his better nature and asked him if he could persuade Ellis to grant me a testimonial for the end of the season as I would then have been at Villa for ten years. It was obviously normal for most clubs to offer a testimonial to a player who had been there ten years or more, especially one who had achieved what I had. I was back in Turner's office two days later. Ellis had agreed.

I was slightly surprised that the chairman agreed, but I have a feeling it might have been because around that time Derby County made an approach to sign me. Ellis probably thought the testimonial would be a good way of encouraging me to leave Villa early to go to

Derby and save him a few quid in wages. There was also interest from Preston, but I didn't want to go into the Third Division, as I thought I was better than that. I spoke to them, though, but it didn't take me long to say no.

The Derby proposal was more appealing because they were a big club, albeit in the Second Division, and the drive from my house near Lichfield wasn't too far, on the A38. Arthur Cox was manager at the time and was well-respected, so the signs were positive. Kevin Maxwell and Stuart Webb came to my house to try to advance the deal. We had a good chat but when the thorny issue of money came up, it took a turn for the worse.

My wages weren't the problem, it was the fact that Ellis was apparently asking for £60,000 for me. I was nonplussed, to put it politely. After ten years at Villa, did Ellis really need to demand a nominal fee for me? I say nominal, which it was to Villa then, but to Derby it was a big deal as they were in the league below and never had great finances to flex. Stuart and Kevin were saying they didn't have a lot of money and were hoping the fee that Ellis was asking for could instead be redirected to me as a signing-on fee and my wages. They asked me if I could persuade Ellis to drop the transfer fee that he was holding out for. 'Leave it with me,' I said.

I arranged the meeting with the chairman and did my best to charm him. 'Derby told me you're asking for sixty grand for me, Mr Chairman. Can I please ask that you allow them to take me on a free so that it allows me to make some money out of this deal, after all the years I have given to the football club? That would be a nice gesture.' He looked at me and said, 'Look, whatever deal I'm discussing with Derby County has got nothing to do with you. You worry about your football and leave the finances to me.'

Ellis's obstinate, and maybe even vindictive, behaviour meant my move to Derby ended right there. I knew he didn't like me and in this conversation he took great delight in slighting me. I guess I represented a successful Aston Villa in the three years he was not at the club and he never got over it. I just thought it was an opportunity for him to be gracious, but I should have known better.

It shouldn't have come as a surprise after the conversation Tony Barton had repeated to me a year earlier. When Ellis initially refused my testimonial, he had apparently told Tony, 'No player at this football club will ever get a testimonial while I'm chairman. Any money that comes through our turnstiles will go to the club, not a footballer.'

My last appearance for Villa was as a substitute for McMahon on 20 October 1984 in a 2-2 draw at home to Norwich. It wasn't the type of swansong to my Villa career I had anticipated. I then had to go back to the reserves, until Sheffield United came in and offered me a loan move and a way out of a sad, unfortunate end to what had been a fantastic decade in the main with a football club I grew to love.

Ian Porterfield was aware of my dire situation at Villa and he asked me to go to Bramall Lane on a month's loan. I didn't know him before then and we had no history together. But one player who was already there who I did have some history with was Phil Thompson. He was a Scouser like me and went to my school, albeit in the year below. My old Villa mate John Burridge was also there, while I knew Mel Eves from our Midlands derbies.

I was happy to agree the move because I was keen to get away from Villa. I didn't dislike playing with the lads in the reserves as it was still a game of football and they were good guys. But I was playing at a level that I knew was beneath me. I knew I was still good enough to play much higher and I hadn't played a first-team game by then for nine weeks. The Blades were 19th when I joined and jumped four places after a nice 4-1 debut victory at home to Alan Ball's Portsmouth, who included a young Neil Webb and my old Villa team-mate Noel Blake. My second match was another home game that brought me up against more familiar faces, as Birmingham City came to Bramall Lane.

It was a 4-3 thriller as Ron Saunders' Blues side took the points. They had Des Bremner, Robert Hopkins, Dave Geddis and my old Coventry City team-mate Brian Roberts. It never felt any less painful losing to the Blues even though I was no longer wearing the claret and blue of Aston Villa.

I built up a decent relationship with the manager, Ian Porterfield. He allowed me to train at Bodymoor

Heath on Monday, Tuesday, Wednesday and Friday. I only trained with Sheffield on a Thursday in a typical week when there was no midweek game. At the end of my one-month loan, their chairman asked me to stay for another month, which I was happy to do because I was just treading water in the Villa reserves.

It was a struggle for the team generally that season, jostling for mid-table. The only match I can recall with any clarity was my last, a competitive Yorkshire derby at home to Barnsley. The result was immaterial. It was more that I had my face smashed by their centre-forward Rodger Wylde. I never knew him, had no history with him, but it didn't stop him from elbowing me with what I would call an illegal challenge, which saw me carried off and needing several stitches to repair my split lips. Wylde didn't even get a yellow card, but he did end up getting sent off that day. I don't know what his problem was. Maybe it was because he was a former Sheffield Wednesday player?

Some local journalists encouraged me to bring charges against Wylde and I didn't need much persuading as I was disgusted by his cowardly act. I had played many tough games of football all through my career against some of the hardest midfielders around like Graeme Souness, Bryan Robson and Billy Bremner, and I had never had my face remodelled before. I never wore shin pads because I wasn't comfortable in them, but I was always adept at avoiding strong tackles when they came. There was no avoiding this swipe, though. I brought a charge of bringing the game into disrepute against Wylde, yet at the hearing at Lancaster Gate they said it was just my word against his due to a lack of evidence. I even had a witness who was a dentist, watching the game, but still it wasn't enough. He got away with it.

After my loan finished, Porterfield told me he would sign me in the summer when I was out of contract. I felt good about that because it gave me a sense of comfort that my career was sorted for at least another season. That move never materialised, though. Ironically, he signed two of my old mates, Peter Withe from Villa and Ken McNaught from West Brom, but not me. I bumped into him the following season at my hotel when they came down to play Brighton. He explained that the chairman wouldn't allow him to sign more older players. So that was that. I would still have appreciated a call to explain but it never came.

So, after my two months at Bramall Lane, it was back to Villa and reserve-team football. It was ironic that I picked up another medal while I was frozen out of the first team. We won the Birmingham Senior Cup with players like Kevin Poole, Ray Walker, Dean Glover, Paul Kerr, Darren Bradley and Tony Daley, before his first-team career took off. I enjoyed playing with the reserves. I would obviously have preferred to be in the first team, but it was still a game of football with a good bunch of lads. Dean Glover was captain and when it was time to pick the trophy up, he said, 'I'm not picking the trophy up, that's your job.' I tried to talk him out of it but he was adamant, so I raised the trophy. It was a nice gesture by Dean.

My very last day as a Villa player was my testimonial against an England XI managed by Bobby Robson. On a nice evening in May, we might usually have seen a crowd of around 15,000 but it was a horrible night after it had rained all day. The weather put the supporters off. Those who did turn out enjoyed the occasion and a few of them ran onto the pitch after the final whistle and piggy-backed me around the ground. That was the ultimate realisation that this was me and Villa done.

There was a tear in my eye as I knew my time at Villa Park was over.

Sussex by the Sea

*'I tipped Graham Turner off about
Dean Saunders at Brighton and said he
could get him on the cheap ... I told him
he would set the Holte End alight and
would make the dressing room a funny
place. He seemed interested but I don't
know if he did anything with my advice'*

I WAS very disappointed that no First Division club came in for me after I was player of the season for Villa the year before. Most people in the game knew that I was always fit to play, as my full season for Brighton went on to show. It does make me wonder whether I was told of all the offers because I later heard that my old Coventry City manager Gordon Milne wanted to sign me for Leicester City but I was never made aware of that interest at the time. I was nonplussed by the way my career was allowed to fizzle out at the top level.

I had an approach from Alan Buckley to go to Walsall on £250 per week, but I wasn't that keen to play in the Third Division and the prospect of playing on that sloping mudheap of a ground at Fellows Park in the middle of winter didn't excite me too much either.

Then an approach came in from my old Coventry team-mate Chris Cattlin, who was in his first managerial job at Brighton & Hove Albion. That offer was worth £400 a week, which was still £200 less than I had been earning at Villa but it didn't seem such a bad idea. No signing-on fee was offered, though Brighton paid my moving costs. I agreed to go to Brighton because of Chris. I only found out when I went down there that they were having a few financial troubles. It seemed like they were having to beg, borrow and steal various things and didn't have their own training ground, but that didn't really affect me.

Chris gave me a two-year contract and I saw the move as something new and fresh, living by the sea in Hove. I asked him about being a player-coach and we had a gentlemen's agreement that we'd get my two years out of the way and would then look at it again. I was happy with that arrangement as I was still feeling fit and good enough for at least the Second Division.

I looked at their squad and it appeared to be really good. They had goals and power upfront with Justin Fashanu, Alan Biley, Terry Connor, Mick Ferguson and a young Dean Saunders. There was Eric Young and Gary O'Reilly at the back, Danny Wilson was the star who made them tick, while there was also Steve Penney, Steve Gatting and a young Martin Keown on loan from Arsenal. It looked a super squad and I was encouraged that they had finished sixth the season before.

Fash didn't play as much as we would have wanted him to because he was injury prone. It was such a shame because he was a force as a centre-forward, a real handful. He was better than Biley, Connor and Ferguson. I would have liked to see Justin playing up front for us a lot more than he did, but he had this knee injury that kept recurring. He reminded me of Peter Withe or Cyrille Regis: big, strong, robust, good on the deck and great in the air of course. Like me, this was his one and only season at Brighton. It was a pity how his situation ended up.

I had an agreement with Chris that when we played at Hove, I would make my own way down there on a Wednesday night and stay until after the match on the weekend. Until I bought a two-bedroom flat in Hove, that is. It was a nightmare of a journey from the West Midlands, so I'd sometimes catch the train, or drive at other times. I would meet the team on the coach on the M1 if we had a game north of Birmingham. Chris looked after me. That I bought property down there shows how excited I was for the move, and I did genuinely feel I could see my career out at the club.

When Jan and the two boys came down to live with me, they loved it as well. The seafront was 100 yards away. I thought playing at Brighton and the potential of a coaching job down the line was all very exciting. The lifestyle there was great.

The initial plan was for me to do my own training at Bodymoor Heath. But I didn't want to go to Bodymoor as the Aston Villa chapter was already over for me and I'd already said my goodbyes to the Villa lads. I was going to train on my own, but I'll be honest, I never did. I didn't do any training when I was at Brighton. I felt like I had trained all my career and didn't want to do it anymore. But I didn't do nothing. I did a lot of walking and was still fit enough to play 49 games that season. I had a resilience built into my system that meant I had done my training over the previous 15 years, so I never felt like I was missing the five-a-sides or fitness drills at training for Brighton.

Before I bought the flat, I stayed at a hotel in Hove for six months. There was also Gavin Oliver and Justin Fashanu staying there. On a typical Friday afternoon, we would go and have a walk on the promenade along with Dean Saunders, who was settled and had his own place, but he would come with us. We'd go and have some pasta and then a leisurely walk along the coastline.

On Thursday nights, myself and Deano would go to the casino. I wasn't a gambler but we'd put 20 quid each into a kitty and Dean would play all the machines to try and win us something back. It wasn't about the gambling for me, we didn't drink, it was just a bit of fun and a good way of spending a night. We'd leave about 10.30 and go our separate ways before training the next day.

I got to know Deano very well and I thought he was a great lad, a real character, even in those early days, and he just fitted in. He was so funny. He did these impressions and the one I can remember better than any was John Bond. He had played under Bondy at Swansea City and even though he was from Wales, he had his London accent down to a tee.

Dean was a fantastic talent as a player and I said to myself that if things don't work out at Brighton and I end up somewhere else, I will tell my new manager to go and get Dean. I wish he had been able to play alongside someone like Peter Withe at that stage of his career because he was so raw that he needed reminding that you don't have to run 100-miles-per-hour chasing balls down every time. He wanted to use that pace he had all the time. He was doing too much running and needed a mentor. Fergie was there, but he was often injured.

When I knew my days at Brighton were numbered the following summer, I met Graham Turner again in a car park after we had both attended a Midlands sports writers' luncheon. Any bad blood between us from Villa was water under the bridge from my point of view. I tipped him off about Dean and said he could get him on the cheap if he went for him then. I told him he would set the Holte End alight and would make the dressing room a funny place. He seemed interested but I don't know if he did anything with my advice.

Dean ended up going to Oxford United shortly after for about £60,000. Villa really missed out there because they ended up spending a couple of million to sign him from Liverpool a few years later. Deano would have saved Turner's job at Villa with his goals and could possibly have led them to more success.

Chris Cattlin got the sack at the end of that season. I think it might have been because he wanted to sell the likes of Perry Digweed, Eric Young and Graham Pearce, who all lived in London and couldn't wait to get back there after training or a match and weren't seen as good mixers with their Brighton team-mates. They didn't want to stick around to do club projects in the community or things like that and Chris was keen to sell them. The club probably felt it was easier to get rid of Chris than all those players.

I saw Chris at a Coventry City Legends' Day in recent years and we got talking about our Brighton days. He said to me, 'I never thanked you.' I said, 'What for?' He said, 'You could have come down to us and been a big-time Charlie having won what you had, but you didn't. You came down and really got stuck in.' I appreciated his comment, but it also made me think, 'That season could have been spent contributing to Aston Villa's cause with a few of my old mates like Kenny Swain and Ken McNaught,' but again, it wasn't to be.

So, with Chris sacked, I was then thinking, 'Who's going to come in and what's going to happen to me?' Barry Lloyd came in from Fulham and took us on a seven-day pre-season tour of Hong Kong, which was my first time there. It was a different world, but a very friendly world with no evidence of animosity or anything to make you feel uncomfortable. I thoroughly enjoyed the trip.

Alan Mullery was appointed manager when we got back and Barry became his number two. I had never met Mullery, yet I saw in a Sunday paper that he criticised the arrangement I had with Chris Cattlin regarding my training days and so on. I was incensed that the new manager was telling the whole world his thoughts on me instead of being man enough to call me in for a meeting to ask me himself what I was all about. It pissed me off quite a bit.

So, on his first day of training, I made a point of going to see him in his office. I asked him, 'Why did you put that piece in the paper? You've not spoken to me or anything! Wouldn't you have been better off having a private chat with me first instead of doing that?' He shrugged as if to say, 'You're probably right.' But the damage was done.

I wondered what he thought of me as a footballer. At the same time, I was trying to work Mullers out as a manager. His first signing was Dale Jasper from Chelsea. He had obviously seen him play, thought a lot of him and felt he could build his team around him. Before I wasted too much time wondering where I fitted in, Mullery called me into his office and told me he was giving me a free transfer. I understood and saw it coming because I hadn't been favoured in any of the pre-season matches. I was past the age of getting angry and banging doors. I just needed to deal with it.

Booed at the Blues

*'I can only imagine the reaction of both
the Birmingham and Villa fans when
they picked up the* Evening Mail *to see
the headline: "Villa Legend Mortimer
Signs for Blues"!'*

ONCE I knew my short-lived Brighton career was over with, I got in touch with my journalist friend Hugh Jamieson and asked him if he could put a piece in the paper saying that Alan Mullery was giving me a free and that I was looking to play for a club in the Midlands, nearer home. He did that article for me and on the Monday afternoon, after it had been published in the Sunday papers, Brian Little phoned me up. Apparently, his chairman had given him permission to speak to me about me joining Wolves. I told him I'd grab my boots from Brighton and would sign straight away. He said, 'Hold your horses, I just needed to know you were interested. Now I know, I'll get back to the chairman and we'll speak again tomorrow.' I was happy at the prospect of joining Wolves and playing for Brian.

I phoned Jan up and said, 'Fingers crossed, I'll be home tomorrow and signing for Wolves.' The next day there was another twist.

I got another call. This time, it was John Bond, the Birmingham City manager, saying he wanted me to sign for him at the Blues. I tried to shut him down and told him I was almost certainly going to be signing for Wolves later that day. But he said, 'I don't know anything about Wolves, but what I do know is that my chairman has given me permission to sign you for Birmingham.' Obviously, as an ex-Villa captain I wasn't that keen to go to Birmingham City. The problem I had, though, was Brian was only caretaker manager at Wolves and didn't have a great deal of authority on transfers. We did speak the next day as planned and Brian intimated something strange was happening because his chairman had gone cold on him at the same time Bondy had been in touch with me.

I was happy to play at Wolves or Blues because it meant I could move back home to the West Midlands and extend my career for at least another season. My preference was Wolves because Brian had mentioned using me as a player-coach. In the end, Brian said he didn't like the way the wind was blowing at Wolves and it was clear that I needed to sign for Blues, which proved a wise decision as he was gone soon after and replaced by Graham Turner. Lucky escape!

I went across to St Andrew's, met with John and signed for them, a few days before the start of the season and my debut at Stoke City. I stayed on the same money

I was on at Brighton. I didn't want to rock the boat by asking for too much or even a signing-on fee, which is why players now have agents! What I should have done was phone Des [Bremner] and asked him for his advice. I'm sure Des would have been on more as he signed for Blues when Ron Saunders was there and Ron would definitely have looked after him.

I can only imagine the reaction of both the Birmingham and Villa fans when they picked up the *Evening Mail* to see the headline: 'Villa Legend Mortimer Signs for Blues'! It was funny because in the starting line-up at Stoke, we had five ex-Villa players as I followed Des, Robert Hopkins, Tony Rees and Mark Jones.

I had a couple of days' training with the lads before my debut and I have to say I fitted in very easily, despite the obvious downsides to my switch to St Andrew's. It was a decent squad. Martin Kuhl was captain and up front was Steve Whitton, who I thought was excellent: strong, could play on his own in attack and was a real handful. It was a good, well-balanced team. There was also former Leicester striker Steve Lynex, Wayne Clarke, a good goalscorer, the ex-Man City right-back Ray Ranson and Julian Dicks was at left-back before he went on to West Ham and then Liverpool.

On my debut at Stoke, when the teams were announced, they got to my name at number 11 and all I could hear was this loud boo from the travelling City supporters. I had a wry smile because it wasn't something I didn't expect, though was probably anticipating it more at home. We won 2-0 and were off to a good start.

I didn't have to wait long for my home debut as it came just two days later on the Bank Holiday Monday, in front of a shockingly low attendance of just over 7,000. We went top of the league with a 2-1 win over Bradford City. I managed to silence a few of the boo-boys by scoring both of our goals after we had gone 1-0 down. It's funny how a goal or two and a few wins can change people's minds as to whether you were a good signing or not. But I knew there would be an element of the Blues support who would never accept me because of where I had been and what I meant to Aston Villa.

Unfortunately, we couldn't sustain our winning start to the season and suffered a couple of bad losing streaks throughout the campaign and ended up only finishing two points above relegated Sunderland.

It was certainly an experience playing for John Bond. He was a larger-than-life figure, but you didn't know which way he was going to blow half the time. Sometimes he was smart, jovial and clever, and at other times he would be loud and come over as being angry. These fluctuations in character were hard to follow because you never knew what mood he would be in. Bondy was the first volatile manager I played under as all the others had been calm or calculated. Chris Cattlin could raise his voice, but he came over in a positive way that sounded inspirational. Even in recent times when I have met him, he's still got that effervescent way. Bondy, though, was very up and down.

We played at Hull City one day and Bondy kept us in the dressing room for about 45 minutes before anyone could get changed and all he was doing was waxing lyrical about our striker Tony Rees. It was embarrassing for Tony actually, while the rest of us were just thinking, 'It's 2.45, when can we get changed and get prepared for this match?' Bondy was going on and on about how great Tony was and how lucky we were to have him in the team. Ok, I get it, he was building his confidence. But at half-time he absolutely slaughtered poor Tony, who had gone from feeling seven feet tall at kick-off to not worthy of wearing the Birmingham City badge at half-time. It was a bit weird. We lost that game 3-2 by the way, after they scored three goals in five minutes straight after half-time. Maybe we were still bemused by Bondy's team talk!

I wouldn't say he was a bad manager because he did clearly have a lot of knowledge on the game, but I wasn't a big fan of his methods because of his Jekyll and Hyde character.

I tried to have an open and honest relationship with him from the start and I told him that at Brighton I only trained with the team one or two days a week because I looked after myself at home, and after the career I'd had, I was more than ready for games on a Saturday afternoon. I explained that I didn't need to train and even with this arrangement, I still played almost 50 games for Brighton. By now, I found training boring.

I know that Birmingham was much closer to my house than Brighton, but it wasn't all about the travel.

I just didn't want to train anymore. We were often playing two games a week as well. I was hoping to get Bondy's approval, but he just said, 'If you want to take the occasional day off, that's fine.' It wasn't the response I had hoped to hear. I knew then I needed to go in every day because he was obviously not keen on me skipping training every week. I thought if this season doesn't go well for me or the team, I'm not going to give him the excuse of me not training being a factor. So, I went in every day.

For the second season running, my manager was sacked at the end of the campaign. John was given the elbow and Gary Pendrey came in as the new Birmingham manager, just as my one-year contract ended.

Alan Buckley phoned me at the end of the season and asked me to play for him at Kettering Town. By this stage, I was not especially bothered that they were non-league, in the Conference. Football is football, it was still a game. I did pre-season training with Birmingham City, though, as it was local. I had verbally agreed with Alan that I would play for him, but I had no contract at that stage.

I actually loved training with Gary Pendrey and I thought he was brilliant. Gary was a players' manager, a bubbly wise-cracking character but someone who knew the game as well. He was more attached to the players, whereas John Bond could be quite aloof. Gary told me he was impressed with my training and sounded me out as to whether I would sign for another year if he could get the chairman to agree. 'Yes of course,' I said, as I hadn't signed anything with Kettering. But I never heard any more from Gary so the chairman obviously never gave him the go-ahead. I would have been happy to have even been a bit-part player and come off the bench to do a job a few times. In the end, I was able to keep my word with Alan Buckley and played for Kettering for six months. That was my Football League career done. Frustratingly, I never did manage 600 league appearances and I would have loved to have done that (I managed 590).

From Redditch to Brazil

*'The PFA called me and said Ellis didn't
want me at the club. It wasn't up to the
PFA guys to ask him why not ... [but] it
was no secret why he didn't want me there'*

I WAS approached by Redditch United about whether
I would be interested in becoming their player-manager
in 1988. They were a couple of divisions below the
Football League but were a well-respected club in the
Midlands non-league scene. It's a job that other former
pros such as Dietmar Bruck, Graham Hyde and Darren
Byfield have held at different times.

I thought they were quite good after watching them
play at Burton Albion, and agreed to take the job. My
first challenge was an interesting one. They had this
midfield star called Simon Berger, who ran the show.
He was fantastic. I wondered why this lad was playing at
such a low level and why this team was struggling with
him in it. The feedback from the general manager was
that his religion was stopping him from playing at the
weekend. I said, 'I'd rather have him half the time for

midweek games than not at all,' and I filled in for him in weekend matches. It was an enjoyable challenge but frustrating. My highest-paid player was earning £30, and if they were offered an extra five quid from another club they would just leave for the extra money. That made it difficult. I did it for over a year until they terminated my contract. I knew we could have done better but the lack of financial resources made it very tough to succeed, especially if you're not an expert at that level. I didn't have long to mope as I was soon off to Brazil!

That I never got to play for my country will always be a frustration, though I had little control over it. Nothing could ever make up for that disappointment. But something I did get to do in January 1989 was play in Brazil for Great Britain Over-35s in the Copa Pele tournament. It was a six-nation event with hosts Brazil, Argentina, Uruguay, Italy, West Germany and us. We came last but managed to beat the Germans 2-1 and drew 0-0 with Italy. Gordon Banks put a squad together that included myself, Alan Kennedy, David Johnson, Terry McDermott, Norman Hunter, Frank Worthington, Gordon Hill, Kenny Burns, Martin Buchan, Don Masson, John Robertson, Peter Osgood, Mick Bates, Joe Corrigan, Peter Bonetti, Alan Whittle and Duncan McKenzie.

There were plenty of household names amongst the opposition as well with Franz Beckenbauer, Paul Breitner, Klaus Augenthaler, Paolo Rossi, Alberto Tarantini and Rivellino. Pele was around as the guest of honour, though he never played.

I couldn't resist going up to Breitner and introducing myself as Dennis Mortimer from Aston Villa. He wasn't too impressed, which seems to be a consistent reaction as I have since heard that his Bayern Munich team expected to just turn up and squash us in Rotterdam. Any mention of that final is a bit of an embarrassment to them, apparently.

We lost a few centre-halves in the first week, so I had to drop back and play with Burnsy in the centre of defence. I would have preferred to play in midfield, but we had a lot of good midfielders anyway, so I didn't mind helping out. The whole thing was an enjoyable experience. It was no surprise Brazil won and it seemed like half of their squad were younger than 35 and still playing. The only disappointing thing was that we couldn't put together enough English players so we could play with an England shirt. We had to come up with a specially made Great Britain jersey with the Union Jack on.

The camaraderie was good. I'm sure we were all missing the game in our retirement so it was good fun to go back into a dressing room environment again and hear the banter flying around amongst the guys. We also managed to play a decent standard of football. We did the tourist bit and took a trip to Rio de Janeiro from Sao Paulo, where the games were being played. We all went up Sugarloaf Mountain on the cable car. It was then that Alan Whittle said, 'That's Ronnie Biggs over there!' – the Great Train Robber being something of a tourist attraction. The cable car ride was in two parts so after the first part you could have your photo with him. Then on the way down from the top you would pick up your item with the photo on, whether you ordered a T-shirt, a mug, a print or whatever. I didn't want my photo with him as I wasn't interested in hero-worshipping someone who was essentially a criminal. I was, though, happy to take Alan's picture with him with my camera when Alan asked me to take one.

My next work opportunity came in October 1989 after the Professional Footballers' Association implemented the government-backed Football in the Community scheme with all 92 Football League clubs involved. Every club was to employ its own community officer to help them connect better with their public. The idea was as much about giving out-of-work footballers a job at a club where they had been popular. Sheffield United, for instance, employed Tony Currie. If clubs could attract ex-players of that calibre, it was obviously going to help the club engage with supporters.

The guys running the scheme at the PFA, who included the ex-Manchester City player Paul Power, called me up to say that Aston Villa were keen to have their officer appointed as soon as possible and they were meeting with Doug Ellis the next day. They said they would get back to me once the meeting was over.

They called me the following evening and said quite abruptly that Ellis told them he didn't want me at the club. It wasn't up to the PFA guys to ask him why not as it was essentially Ellis's club – he would just have told them he can employ who he wants. It was no secret why he didn't want me there, though I had hoped Ellis would have been big enough to swallow his pride and not see me as a reminder of the successful three years when he wasn't at the football club, but obviously he was incapable of doing that.

I thought the captain of the Villa team which won the league championship and European Cup would make a great ambassador for the club. I was surprised Ellis was vindictive enough to deny me this role at Aston Villa. I was never a fan of his, but I had never crossed swords with him either. I saw this job as the perfect way to reconnect with Villa and eventually join the coaching staff. That Ellis blocked my path really got up my nose and I thought, 'I don't like this man.' I promised myself then that I would use any opportunity I had to criticise him in public about the things he did which were not in the best interests of Aston Villa. Like how he never had one photograph of the European Cup team around the club when he was chairman.

I was later a willing participant in anti-Ellis movements and protests, especially with the supporters' group, Villa Fans Combined, which was set up to try to oust him as Villa chairman. My involvement created a few headlines and one time they had planned a march I was working for the PFA at the time. I was asked by our boss Gordon Taylor not to participate in the march after he had received a call 'from Aston Villa' though we all know who was behind that call. I had no intention of marching anyway, but it was interesting that Ellis was rattled enough to call up Gordon Taylor.

Back to 1989. The PFA guys were surprised by the development at Villa but knew they had to move on as Ellis wasn't going to change his mind about me. They told me they were going into West Brom the next day and the club wanted someone in place right away. The PFA had nobody in mind because to get one of these jobs you had to be a Level 4 coach and be an ex-player – preferably an ex-player of that particular club – but no West Brom players were on their radar, so they proposed my name. The West Brom manager Brian Talbot and the club secretary were happy for me to join them so I was offered the job as West Bromwich Albion's community officer, which I accepted.

In case you're wondering when I started my training to be a coach, it was actually in the same season as Villa won the league. Myself, Peter Withe and David Geddis went to a venue in Wolverhampton for six consecutive Sundays in November and December to help us qualify as a Level 2 coach and get on the ladder in football coaching. We would play against the likes of Kenny Dalglish and Bryan Robson on Saturdays and then mingle with schoolteachers and Sunday team coaches on Sundays. It was just something that we were all very ambitious to achieve and we followed that by attending the A Licence two-week residential course at Lilleshall. We didn't do any coaching then until we finished our playing careers but knew that one day it would stand us in good stead, as was the case.

I enjoyed the role at West Brom, but I was happier once I was appointed reserve-team manager there. That came about once Osvaldo Ardiles took over as manager after Talbot's departure. Ossie and I weren't exactly friends but I like to think we had a healthy respect for one another having played against each other for a few years. He had managed Swindon Town and Newcastle United before he took this job and he seemed to make a shrewd decision when bringing his former Tottenham boss Keith Burkinshaw to The Hawthorns with him as his assistant. Ossie wasn't a great communicator with the players with his broken English but that's where Keith stepped in to help him out. Keith was good with the players.

I had been at West Brom for three years as community officer by the time Ossie came to the club and I was ready for a new challenge. A lot of staff had moved on when Talbot left so there were a few vacancies. I tapped on Ossie's door to ask if he would consider me as the reserve-team manager. That turned out to be a productive decision as I was there in his office for two hours as he grilled me about the first-team squad. I used to watch all the Albion home games so I had a good idea about the players, like Bob Taylor, Bernard McNally and Darren Bradley. It wasn't long after that Ossie offered me the position. I was now doing what I wanted to be doing, working with players rather than hosting schools or junior teams at The Hawthorns, which wasn't a bad job but just not as rewarding as being a coach.

West Brom worked out well for Ossie and his diamond formation as he only stayed one season and won promotion to the second tier via the play-offs. He was then offered the job he couldn't turn down, which took him back to his beloved Tottenham Hotspur. Keith had obviously been there and done that, so he took on the manager's job and made me his assistant.

I loved that role. It was exactly what I wanted to be doing. I never craved being a manager myself. What I did enjoy, though, was coaching footballers, especially at the highest possible level. We had some good players to work with and there was even talk for a while that Kevin Donovan could play for England but, unfortunately, he wasn't able to kick on.

We had a tough season back in the second tier and won 1-0 at Portsmouth on the last day of the 1993/94 season to survive. Being a coach leaves you in a constant state of deliberating with yourself and after a poor performance it's not unusual to think, 'Was that my fault or did the players let me down?' It was the players usually but it's only normal to doubt yourself as a coach and question whether you could have done anything different to better affect the outcome.

Ossie and Keith had this routine where they would hold a post-match meeting, usually on the Monday morning, to review the match they had just played. It certainly wasn't something I was used to with Ron Saunders at Villa. I preferred to air any views there and then and move on. A couple of months before Keith and myself were sacked in October 1994, we played a two-legged League Cup tie against Hereford United. We drew 0-0 in the first leg at Edgar Street and I was fuming and knew I would struggle to wait until the meeting to express my thoughts on what I had just seen. I was more annoyed by the blasé behaviour of some of the players, who were getting changed in a bubbly mood. I told Keith, 'Sorry mate, but I need to say something here,' and he gave me his blessing. I said, 'I don't know why some of you are in a jovial mood because what I just witnessed out there wasn't good enough. Don't be thinking it will be any easier when it comes to the second leg at our place. It will be far from it!' I was probably only aiming those words at three or four players but sometimes it's best to speak to the team than pointedly turn to one player and give him an earful. I think Ian Hamilton and Kevin Donovan were two I was referring to. It was no surprise to me when Hereford won the return leg 1-0 and knocked us out. We were bottom of the league at the time as well, so it wasn't a great time for us.

The nadir came at Tranmere Rovers' Prenton Park on 15 October 1994. Keith was watching from the directors' box, but I always preferred the dugout. It was one of those games where nothing seemed to go right for us. We were 2-1 down at half-time before John Aldridge completed his hat-trick for them just after the break. That's how it finished, 3-1. I noticed after half-time when I turned round that the chairman Trevor Summers was sitting next to me on the bench. It was a strange moment in time. I gave him a bit of a quizzical look as if to say, 'What the fuck are you doing here?'

He looked at me and snapped: 'Get 'em going for God's sake!'

I said, 'Mr Chairman, we're not playing bad. Anyway, I can't score goals for them or defend for them. That's up to the players.'

I spoke to Keith afterwards and he said, 'One minute the chairman was sitting next to me and then he was gone. Next thing I saw, he was sitting next to you in the dugout.'

That was really weird. I've never known a chairman who went down to the touchline like that to speak to the manager. Not even Doug Ellis!

It should have come as no surprise that we were sacked after that match, though I was probably the last person to be told. Keith still lived in Hertfordshire then so he would join us on a Monday after I took training in the morning. I was taking training at 11 o'clock on the Monday morning with no inkling that the sack was coming. We got inside to be greeted with 'Burkinshaw Sacked' headlines. That was the first I knew of anything changing. Keith never told me that he knew it was coming, if he had in fact been told the night before.

I was eventually asked to go into the boardroom where I was also sacked. I looked at Tony Hale and said, 'Why are you sacking me?' He replied: 'The number twos always go with the manager.' I said, 'No they don't!' I wasn't prepared to get into an argument with him and just asked him what they were going to pay me, as I was 18 months into a four-year contract. My salary was only £30,000 and they agreed to pay me £25,000 ex-gratia. Alan Buckley and his staff were appointed very soon after we left so I was sure they had been tapped up while Keith and myself were still in our jobs.

So, there I was, jobless. I asked the PFA what should be my next move? They said, 'You need to sign on the dole.' I thought they were joking but they weren't, so I followed their recommendation and went down to my local job centre and filled out all the forms and answered their questions. They told me to come back in a week. On the Wednesday night, that following week, I was asked to do some match summarising for BBC Radio WM, which I did for just £60 because it was football and I saw any involvement as a positive as you never know where it might lead.

Anyway, the next morning, I walked into the dole office and saw the clerk. The first thing he said was, 'Were you on the radio last night?' I said, 'Yeah.' He said, 'Were you paid?' I said, 'Yeah.' He said, 'So what are you doing here?' I said, 'Oh so that's how it works? You're expected to live on sixty quid a week?' That was the end of my brief association with the job centre. I remember walking out thinking, 'Why did I allow the PFA to talk me into this?' I guess nowadays, people in the queue would be tweeting that a former Villa player is signing on!

I did a few years with Radio WM in the end. I like to think I was very honest but not everyone appreciated my honesty and there was a headline one time that I had been banned from Aston Villa Football Club. It made for a good story, but the actual truth was that I had been banned from the reception area behind the North Stand where we used to pick up our passes and the players and staff would come in through the same entrance. They didn't want to see me apparently because of the criticisms I made on occasions. I have a feeling the manager at the time was my old team-mate, John Gregory. The ban would have been more to do with Ellis, though, who wouldn't have had much hesitation in banning me. I took satisfaction that I was obviously getting under his skin.

My next 'proper' job was again with the PFA, as the regional director of coaching in the Midlands. They determined that the 'YTs' (youth training scheme scholars) needed an official certificate at the end of their two years so even if they weren't retained by the club they were at, they at least had a qualification that could enable them to work in football. I was always telling the boys that what they were doing – a Level 2 course – could mean they might end up working in America as a coach if their playing careers didn't work out. We also helped the pros do their Level 3 coaching courses to prepare them for coaching careers if that was the direction they wanted to go in.

I also had a year at the Blues as a community officer before a six-year stint with the Football Association, coaching coaches at the Level 4 stage. We did have quite a few famous names cross our path on these courses. One name that springs to mind who failed the course is ex-Leicester City manager Nigel Pearson. Every now and then we had a group that didn't fathom the assessment part of the course. It's not just about getting out on the training ground and running a session – the assessments were an important aspect. I could never pass someone on reputation because they were a good player. We needed to know they would be good when coaching young footballers, or even experienced ones, so I guess I was quite strict like that.

One of the most interesting days I had in my coaching tuition days was when I hired a room out at Villa Park for my class. On arrival I was told by the young lady that we were in 'The Paul McGrath Suite'. I thought 'Oh, right'. On that corridor I discovered each suite was named after a Villa legend or a famous Villa captain, but as I curiously spied the name on each door, I never did see one with my name on or for that matter any of my mates from the 1982 team. I thought, 'He's done it again, hasn't he!'

Life Beyond Football

'Pete Waterman asked me if I wanted to DJ a set at Mr George's in Coventry city centre. I thought about it for about five seconds and concluded my manager was not going to like his young midfielder flipping vinyl at the local nightspot'

YOU'LL BE aware by now that boozing, golfing or playing darts after training wasn't my thing. I was a family man but also very much into the arts. Maybe that made me a bit different to most footballers but that was just me. That was who I was, who I am now. I never felt like I needed to do things just to be part of something. I loved playing football, I enjoyed the lads and the dressing room camaraderie, but once we were done with training or a game, I often did my own thing.

I've already told you that I was an avid reader of books and especially crime and spy novels. My interest in the arts never ended there. I developed a voracious appetite for music, which has never left me, and I also used to enjoy photography.

I got into photography towards the latter stage of my Coventry career but more so once I arrived at Villa. I got to know the professional photographers who covered my career. Therefore, I was fortunate that over the years I have been given hundreds of images from my career at the various clubs. I spoke to Ken McNaught recently and learned that he doesn't have any photographs from his career, but I guess that's normal. It's only because I showed an interest in photography that I developed these relationships.

I was good friends with Bob Thomas, who used to live in Northampton and he had his own darkroom there. His parents were big Villa fans, so I got to know him. I would go to his house and watch him develop his own photographs in his darkroom. It fascinated me, and when I moved into my current house in 1980, I turned a walk-in wardrobe into my own darkroom. Photography then was a great hobby. I felt I needed a hobby away from football and this was something I really enjoyed doing. I went to the Formula One at Silverstone, the RAC Rally at Sutton Park, and I would go down to Edgbaston cricket ground to take photos of either Warwickshire or England and the touring teams of the year.

I got really involved with it and put together a decent portfolio of black and white photographs – not with any commercial ambitions, just for myself. I only wish I had started it ten years earlier when I toured countries like America, Japan and South Korea with Coventry and then those European trips with Villa, which I didn't make enough of either. If I had been commercially savvy, I would now have a great photographic book of my career on my hands!

I found that taking good photographs was very rewarding. I took it quite seriously. In fact, when my good mate Kenny Swain was captain of Villa for the day against Tottenham when I was injured, I sat next to Villa's official club photographer Terry Weir and tried to learn from him. My first camera was an Olympus OM1, though I was aware the professional sports photographers spent a lot more money than me, on Nikons or Canons.

Terry took some great photos for me with my camera when we were on the open-top bus celebrating winning the league in 1981. I don't understand why I didn't do the same on the bus a year later when we were celebrating winning the European Cup. I saw on a photo in recent times that Andy Blair had a camera around his neck, so I called and asked him what happened to those photos or negatives. He said he only took his camera because he knew I had taken mine a year earlier. Unfortunately, Andy couldn't locate the negatives when I asked if I could scan them.

I took down my darkroom when my second son, Jon, was born in September 1983 as we needed more space. Richard had been born three years earlier so the family was expanding, and space was precious! I found I never had as much time to spend on my photography as I once did. The joys of parenthood! There was a time when I thought I would like to become a sports photographer when I retired but those aspirations fizzled out and I became a coach instead. Boring I know, but football was what I knew after all.

So where did my love of music come from? Well, it never started at home in Liverpool. It wasn't until I got down to Coventry that I realised how great music was.

I was a first-year apprentice and Graham Paddon was a third year. The first team had their own dressing room and the other one was shared by the reserves and the apprentices, so we all got to know each other. I never had a genre or any favourite type of music growing up, so my tastes were a blank canvas then.

My only experience of music in my childhood was when Dad played music on the record player at home, but usually it would be records from Woolworths that were cover versions. I remember *Love Me Do* by The Beatles being played, but this version wasn't *by* The Beatles. It was from some cheap label that copied the hits of the day.

I wasn't into music at that stage of my life, though. It was all about getting outside with my mates and playing football. There was no television then, I didn't listen to the radio, so I wasn't exposed to much music. That changed in Coventry thanks to Graham. He said to me once, 'You really need to listen to The Temptations.' This was a new world he was talking to me about now. That conversation really struck a chord with me and I went into one of the record shops in Coventry and spent some of my hard-earned seven pounds a week on The Temptations' *Greatest Hits*. Then, I just needed something to play it on. It's no good buying records if you can't hear it. I managed to get my hands on a Dansette, with a speaker at the front, which held about ten LPs, and they played them one after the other. They're quite fashionable now.

I immediately took to this sound of Motown and thought, 'I need to know more about this.' I was late to the party, but I soon discovered it was founded by Berry Gordy Jr as Tamla Records on 7 June 1958. It grew to become the huge label that we know it as today.

I bought magazines like *Blues and Soul* and read up on it as much as I could. I still have about 170 copies. Remember, I'm a born collector: the comics, the autographed photos of my Liverpool football heroes; then, once I was a bit older the LPs and music magazines took over. Stamps passed me by, but I revelled in the collection of music. I loved collecting generally, but music gave me so much pleasure.

Even nowadays, I listen to my mix tapes every day on my MP3 player in my car or in the house. I recorded lots of my favourite mix tapes. I found that on so many albums there might be three or four good tracks, but the others were not so good or at least to my taste. Once you split them, every track is something you love. It wasn't always so easy to listen to music in my early days at my digs in Coventry. It was ok once I had my record player and I only wish the Sony Walkman had come out ten years earlier! It really helped me to relax before matches if I couldn't sleep.

There was another movement in England called Northern Soul, which centred around places like Wigan Casino. I never got into the scene while it was new at the time, but if I never moved to the Midlands and had remained in Kirkby then I am sure I would have got into it. Northern Soul was like the Motown movement of the UK.

It was through music that I befriended the famous producer Pete Waterman, who went on to make pop stars of the likes of Kylie Minogue, Jason Donovan, Mel & Kim and so many others. In those days he wasn't famous. I used to go to this clothes shop in Coventry and I could hear music coming from a cellar that was based in this shop. Pete had a record shop down there and we gradually got to know one another.

When he found out I was a footballer with Coventry he was kind enough to send a couple of LPs to my house, though I don't know how he got to find out my address. He sent me records by Harold Melvin & The Blue Notes and The Isley Brothers, which I later found out was their 11th album called *3 + 3*. These artistes started to make an entrance into the British soul music scene and disco. Those couple of albums had a huge influence on me. I still remember one track on that Harold Melvin album, going 'Life is a Cabaret'. I thought, 'What the bloody hell is this all about?' But then listening to more of it, I loved it. There is a track on there now, which remains possibly my favourite song of all time, 'The Love I Lost'. I'm sure I would have got to know about it anyway, but it was Pete who first introduced me to it. That became an iconic song in the disco scene. There are several versions of it – and I love them all.

Talking of Pete, I almost moonlighted as a footballer when he asked me if I wanted to DJ a set at Mr George's in Coventry city centre. I thought about it for about five seconds and concluded my manager was not going to like his young midfielder flipping vinyl at the local nightspot. So that was my DJ career done and dusted there and then.

Despite my love of music, I never did play an instrument. Dad brought home a guitar a few times when he was managing The Denims, but it just never interested me then as me and my brothers were so much into football. Had we gone along to watch the band, then maybe, just maybe, one of us might have gone down that path.

My sons are quite musical, though. My eldest, Richard, plays the piano, guitar, drums and bass. He's very talented and can listen to a track once and make a pretty good attempt at playing it on his bass straight after. My youngest, Jon, played drums for a while and was in a band with his brother and couple of others but they soon lost interest and it fizzled out. My love of music hopefully influenced them in some small way, but I can't take all the credit because Jan has always been quite adept on the piano. We bought a piano many years ago and she still plays it.

Here is a flavour of some of my favourite albums – the Tracks of My Years:

The Impressions – *Big Sixteen, Vol. 1* (1965)

The Temptations – *Greatest Hits* (1966)

The Four Tops – *Greatest Hits* (1967)

Marvin Gaye – *What's Going On* (1971)

Isaac Hayes – *Black Moses* (1971)

Bobby Womack – *Understanding* (1972)

Harold Melvin & The Blue Notes – *Black and Blue* (1973)

The Isley Brothers – *3 + 3* (1973)

Lamont Dozier – *Out Here on My Own* (1973)

Stevie Wonder – *Innervisions* (1973)

Earth, Wind & Fire – *I Am* (1979)

Curtis Mayfield – *Something to Believe In* (1980) – like winning the league championship for the first time in 71 years!

Michael Jackson – *Thriller* (1982)

Maze Featuring Frankie Beverly – *Live in Los Angeles* (1984)

George Michael – *Listen Without Prejudice Vol. 1* (1990)

Teddy Pendergrass – *A Little More Magic* (1993)

Quincy Jones – *'Q's' Jook Joint* (1995)

Prince – *One Nite Alone (Box Set)* (2002)

Luther Vandross – *'Live' Radio City Music Hall* (2003)

Michael McDonald – *Motown Two* (2004)

My Greatest Aston Villa XI

(... don't expect too many surprises!)

THIS WILL get tongues wagging! I know I'm biased as I was captain of the Villa team that won the league championship and European Cup, but nobody can change the simple fact that this side won major trophies. It's fair to question – after I commented in this book that the Villa team of 1976/77 should have won the treble – why I haven't picked Andy, Giddy or Brian, but that side ultimately won a League Cup and reached the quarter-finals of the UEFA Cup, so the achievements don't compare. If we had gone on to the final and won, then this team might have been different.

I don't know any of the players from yesteryear like **Peter McParland**, **Johnny Dixon** or **Jimmy Dugdale**, so I have only picked players I saw. I've found this task much easier than I would have done if I was asked to pick a Liverpool All-Time XI, because I saw the Shankly team of the 1960s and then played against those great Liverpool teams of the 1970s and 1980s. That would have been very difficult.

There is no place in the team or on my bench for **Paul McGrath**, which will no doubt surprise quite a few people. I felt Paul McGrath was a myth. The word 'legend' is attached too easily today to players. Paul became a big favourite at Villa Park, yet he didn't add to Villa's trophy count besides a couple of League Cups, not one of the big ones. I don't think any of the '82 team were afforded the same God-like qualities McGrath seemed to accrue with the fans, we just became the greatest Villa 'TEAM' ever. This is why Evans and McNaught get into my best team ahead of McGrath. I realise that won't be a popular opinion, but it's my opinion.

Nigel Spink is unlucky not to find a place in the squad but how do I fit him in ahead of Jimmy and Bozzie? **Gareth Barry, Mark Walters, Tony Dorigo** were all good players, but I couldn't fit them in. I also liked the way **Juan Pablo Angel** played at Villa and I'm not sure we got the best out of him. **Christian Benteke** was outstanding at Villa and strangely went away and became a nonentity.

Some fans will probably wonder why I have omitted **Jack Grealish.** I accept he was excellent at Villa, but he is an individual that doesn't fit into a team. The players who I have in my line-up are all team players. They contribute wholly to the team, whereas I find that Grealish is an individual who just likes to do his own thing and wasn't a team player as such. I see team players as those who can get back and defend for his team when they're not in attack. Andy Gray and Brian

Little could defend, even Tony Morley to a lesser degree. Grealish can't defend. I believe his early struggles at Manchester City prove what I'm saying here. I don't think City needed him and maybe they only bought Jack to stop other teams from having him? If he stays a few seasons at City and develops his game, he might prove me wrong. I hope he does.

Dennis Mortimer's Best Aston Villa XI:

1) Jimmy Rimmer – an experienced goalkeeper, unflustered, a good communicator, good shot-stopper. Although he didn't play lots of first-team games at other clubs before coming to Villa, he played a significant part in what we achieved in the early 1980s.

2) Kenny Swain – an outstanding athlete, tremendous energy, a good passer of the ball, strong in defence, very quick and a great attacking player. He was as good as Giddy going forward but had better defensive abilities, understanding his role well and was an integral part of our great team.

3) Gary Williams – defensively was stronger than Gibbo (Colin Gibson) but he seemed to combine better with Tony Morley, supporting him in a defensive way that enabled Tony to attack the opposition defence. Gary didn't try to take Tony's role and run past him.

4) Allan Evans – Allan was slightly different to Ken in the way he approached the role of centre-half, probably because he used to be a centre-forward. He had a great partnership with Ken, could pass a ball, was a solid defender and scored some important goals.

5) Ken McNaught – he really seemed to enjoy his role and was a true defender and liked the battles every week. You knew you could rely on him to do the job that was expected of him. An intelligent defender as well. Scored some useful goals, too.

6) **Dennis Mortimer** – I tried to lead by example. I was prepared to get forward an awful lot and I saw that as a big part of my game. I enjoyed linking up with Gary Shaw and Peter Withe and without them I don't think I would be in this team. Before the 1980/81 side began to blossom, the way I liked to play wasn't really happening as I would have liked. But thankfully things changed with the combination Ron settled on.

7) **Des Bremner** – a tireless runner, the perfect replacement for Frank Carrodus – both were thoroughbreds in terms of their work-rate. He enjoyed getting stuck in, never let us down, even filled in at the centre of defence on occasions and never gave anything less than 100 per cent. Very underrated by the fans but never by the players.

8) **Gary Shaw** – a very creative striker who provided opportunities for me and other midfielders to link up with him. His partnership with Peter was tremendous and they fed off each other. Gary was also a terrific goalscorer and I liken him to Kenny Dalglish in the calm and clinical way that he finished. If it wasn't for his injuries, he would have become an England player and a much bigger name, especially outside of Birmingham.

9) **Peter Withe** – I enjoyed playing with him; he had the ability to hold players off through his height and power. He was a left-footed centre-forward and that was a good trait for him to have as there were not many around like that. He gave us something a bit special and that was the ability to dictate the way matches would go, as he could boss defences.

10) Gordon Cowans – he had a great appreciation of when and how to pass the ball and where to. So many of us, like myself, Des, Tony and Kenny Swain, relied on Gordon's vision to pick a pass with either foot as he could put the ball into a gap exactly where you needed it. He was also a good, strong tackler for someone so slight. Gordon was the complete player with two good feet, a great passer, scored goals and defended well. There's no doubt he was the best player I ever played with.

11) Tony Morley – a great dribbler, was two-footed so he could turn the defender either way, which was always difficult for any full-back marking him. A great lad and a terrific character to have around the dressing room. He never let us down.

Substitutes:
12) Colin Gibson – could be irrational at times, which clouded his decision-making on the odd occasion when the red mist came over. Going forward he was better than Gary Williams, though, and was a great wide-man and crosser.

13) Andy Gray – knew his job and loved playing that leading role up front. He was only my height, 5ft 10in, but had a big leap and was great in the air. He knew how to put the ball in the back of the net or when to lay the ball off. His left-footed ability also helped him. He had everything a centre-forward would want, could score goals, was quick, fit and loved being a target man. His bigger successes came away from Villa (at Everton).

14) John Gidman – Giddy was similar to Kenny Swain in the way he liked to attack down the right-hand side and cross the ball. He had a lot of energy and gave us a real attacking threat, but I just think Kenny Swain enjoyed the art of defending a bit more.

15) Brian Little – very similar to Gary Shaw in the way that he liked to caress the ball into the back of the net. A quality footballer who didn't get the recognition he deserved and if he didn't suffer with injuries he would have achieved much more.

16) David Platt – a terrific scorer of goals from midfield and he made the kind of runs that Des Bremner would make down the right side of the middle, but Platty had the ability to finish better than Des. The link-up play between David and Gordon Cowans was very important during his time at Villa and I don't think he would have been as successful as he was if it weren't for the great passing ability of Gordon.

17) Chris Nicholl – he gave you everything and there was very little missing in his game that you would want in a centre-half. Fearless both in his own box and the attacking box, a great character whose company I enjoyed very much, he led by example as a captain. I always felt with Chris in the team that it was going to be a difficult afternoon for the opposition centre-forwards. He's very unlucky not to make my final XI.

18) Mark Bosnich – had great confidence, there was a security about him. If I was a defender in front of him, I wouldn't feel nervous with him behind me. Emi Martinez is the same now. I am not as big a fan of his as some, as I think he wastes too much time, but I see the security factor he brings. Bosnich, though, exuded confidence and I saw him make many great saves for Villa.

Memories of Morty

*Recollections from some of Dennis's
former team-mates, opponents, managers
and other friends in the game:*

Des Bremner (*Aston Villa & Birmingham City
team-mate*)
'He has always been a nice, honest bloke, very upfront
and never frightened to air his views and he was a true
professional as a footballer who put great emphasis on
his fitness.

'Dennis scored more goals than I did but he was
that sort of player who used to love to go on a run and
have a shot. I'd be there to cover for him if the move
broke down. We knew one another's games inside out
and it was always a pleasure to play alongside him.'

Jim Brown (*Coventry City, club historian*)
'I watched Dennis from the youth team in 1969 and
saw his development into one of the most outstanding
midfield players of that era. He had a great motor, had
a powerful shot and he could attack players and operate

either out on the right or through the middle. He was the epitome of the 1970s box-to-box midfielder.

'It was really sad when he left Coventry because he was the star of the team by then, along with Tommy Hutchison. If it wasn't bad enough him going, we sold him to our local rivals, the Villa! In all seriousness, though, that sale was inevitable as Villa were a bigger club and Dennis deserved a greater stage than we could offer him at Coventry City.

'I have got to know Dennis well over the years, he's a lovely guy and I have always enjoyed our chats together about football and his career.'

John Burridge (*Aston Villa team-mate*)
'He was a fabulous midfield player, a great captain and a great lad, too. Quite honestly, I couldn't tell you who was better between Dennis and Bryan Robson. He was that good. Robbo ended up with 90 caps and Dennis didn't get one! Very unlucky. To be fair, though, there were lots of terrific English midfield players around then, unlike now!'

Willie Carr (*Coventry City team-mate*)
'I'm a bit older than Dennis and subsequently got into the first team before him. I could see early on though that he had good ability, was especially good at running with the ball, was very strong, could go past people and was hard to knock off the ball. He was a nice, quiet lad as well. That first impression of Dennis stayed with me throughout our parallel careers, even when I went

to Wolves and he left for Villa. I always saw him as a very strong, classy footballer running with the ball from midfield.

'I remember when we went on tour to America in the early 1970s, we had all this spending money for our food and drink and most of the lads would enjoy a day out on the beer. But Dennis was never a drinker and I seem to recall him spending all his money on LPs because he liked his music, especially Motown, which I loved as well. There was a strong drinking culture in those days because that's what everybody did, but Dennis was never into that scene, so he was probably ahead of his time in terms of being a professional in the way the game went in modern times.'

Mick Coop (*Coventry City team-mate*)
'Dennis was a good team-mate, who liked to get forward from the right side of midfield then support the strikers. I wouldn't say he was very defensive-minded. At Coventry in those days, every season always seemed like a battle against relegation, apart from the season when we qualified for Europe under Mr Cantwell. Dennis was an important part of those scraps, very hard-working and a real good player who obviously went on to great things at Aston Villa.'

Allan Evans (*Aston Villa team-mate*)
'When I got to Villa in 1977, the captain Chris Nicholl was leaving for Southampton and his successor Leighton Phillips left a year later (to Swansea). It seemed natural

and inevitable to me that Dennis would step up into the captain's role. He was always well thought of, not a guy who rants and raves a lot and he led by example perfectly.

'He had an all-round game, worked hard, could make a challenge and get forward. But the one thing that stood out for me was his consistency – you knew what you were going to get from him virtually every game.

'As a guy I appreciated how Dennis lived his life because we were both non-drinkers, though he was probably less social than I was. When you're captain, you can't be too social. He picked his times when he went out with the lads and did so rarely. That's the way a captain should act. Dennis didn't see he needed to change his character to fit in.'

Trevor Francis (*Birmingham City, Nottingham Forest & England*)
'I well remember playing against Dennis during his days at Coventry and early on in his career at Villa when I was at Birmingham. We always used to reckon at St Andrew's that Howard Kendall was the best player never to play for England. I think that even Howard would concede that title to Dennis Mortimer.

'A strident force for Villa, he has always been a real inspiration to the team. I would say he was undoubtedly the most important player in the team when Villa won the league championship and the European Cup.'

** an excerpt from Dennis's testimonial brochure*

Brian Little (*Aston Villa team-mate*)

'Dennis was one of those classic midfield players that you don't see much of now, who could run with the ball. He was unbelievably powerful when he went on those runs from midfield. His strength was the way he took the ball past people in the middle of the park and committed defenders, and quite often played nice balls through to the forwards. I can think of several occasions when he set goals up for me, notably the League Cup semi-final replay against QPR (in 1977). That was Dennis at his best, bursting past players and within a few seconds he was five yards the other side of them.

'In recent years Jack Grealish had the ability to dribble past defenders, but Dennis used to go past players with similar ease but not by dribbling, he just ghosted past them. He was so talented and quite unique. I can't think of too many like him.

'He was a good leader and a good organiser on and off the pitch as well. I have always had huge respect for him.'

Terry McDermott (*Kirkby Boys district team and regular opponent at Liverpool*)

'We were great in that Kirkby Boys team, me, Dennis, Kenny Swain, John McLaughlin and the other boys. It was terrific fun, we were the best young team in the area.

'When I eventually went to Bury, who I'd never heard of by the way, I seem to recall Dennis was the last one of us to get signed by a league club and that's surprising because he was a great young player. He went on to have a fantastic career with Coventry and Aston Villa.

'He was a very, very good player. He was as good as any of us who played for England at that time but he never got picked, which was very unlucky for him because he deserved it. He really should have played for his country – and I mean that sincerely.'

Ken McNaught (*Aston Villa team-mate*)
'I guess myself and Dennis were the leaders of the group in the Villa team. The difference was Dennis was very quiet and led by example perfectly, while I was a bit more verbal.

'Ron Saunders gave me his blessing that if there were problems – on or off the field – to sort them out. Often you don't have time to wait till half-time out on the park. As regards to away from the pitch, if ever we felt the atmosphere wasn't quite right, we would go out in the afternoon over The Belfry (five minutes from the training ground). Once the alcohol started to work, the younger lads like Sid, Gibbo and the rest would slowly start to say what they weren't happy with. Then, we were able to fix any issues. Dennis wasn't always there because he wasn't a drinker. But if ever you wanted the model professional as a captain to show the way, Dennis was the man.

'He was a fantastic midfield player who linked up superbly with the front men. He had a great instinct to know when a break was on and when to make his run from midfield that would be hard for the opposing midfield or defenders to stop.

'I used to have to tell him, though, when we played against Ipswich that he needed to get back more and sit in front of the defence. Eric Gates played in the hole behind Alan Brazil and Paul Mariner and could give us problems. Dennis never liked playing too deep, but he would ultimately do what was right for the team. We laugh about it now!'

Gordon Milne (*Coventry City manager*)
'Every club could do with a couple of Dennis Mortimers coming through their youth ranks every season to maintain standards.

'It is a pity he didn't get a full international cap to complete his honours. However, he has been excellent for the game, and I am pleased the game has been good to him. What's more, he has done a tremendous job for Villa.'

* an excerpt from Dennis's testimonial brochure

Tony Morley (*Aston Villa team-mate*)
'He would have to be Aston Villa's greatest ever captain. Some captains scream and shout. Dennis wasn't like that. He just did the job and you followed his example. He was quite inspirational. How he never got an England cap is beyond me. He shouldn't have just got a single cap either, he was good enough to play 30 or 40 times for his country. I couldn't think of a better uncapped player.

'He was skilful but could look after himself, not just against tough oppositions but in those conditions that we used to play in back in the day with the mud and snow. I don't know another player capable of making those signature 40–50 yard runs of his, through the mud all game, time and again. I can't remember him ever being less than a seven out of ten; always consistent.

'As a bloke, he was a great lad. Some might say he was boring because he didn't drink or go out much with the lads, but I liked and admired him for who he was. That's why he was a great captain. His manager knew he wasn't going to get a phone call at 2am about his captain drunk in a nightclub. Dennis was the perfect leader of our Villa team.'

Jimmy Rimmer (*Aston Villa team-mate*)
'Dennis is one of the best players I ever played with and I played with a lot of top footballers at Manchester United, Arsenal and Villa. He should have got an England cap, that's for sure.

'At Villa, Dennis, Gordon Cowans and Des Bremner were absolutely brilliant in our midfield. I don't think there was a better midfield in the league at that time. They knew how to play together, two got forward and one stayed back to cover. If ever any of them got injured we then had a problem because, without being rude to the other lads, there was never any reserve in the same class as those guys.

'Dennis made us tick as a team and the only thing that probably stopped him from being an England player was that he didn't score enough goals.

'He didn't speak a lot but was a leader in his own way. Off the field, he would have a drink with the lads but then he would leave soon after and go home. There was nothing wrong with that as that was who he was.'

Brian Roberts (*Coventry City and Birmingham City team-mate*)

'He was a superstar at Coventry by the time I played with him. Good-looking lad with thick, dark hair, like a film star, brilliant footballer who always had time on the ball. He was elegant as a player but then again, I was a defender so everyone other than the goalkeeper was elegant to me!

'I played with Dennis years later when he joined Birmingham and I don't remember him receiving too much stick from the supporters despite him being a Villa legend and that probably speaks volumes as the Blues fans clearly appreciated him as a player, rightly so.'

The late Ron Saunders (*Aston Villa manager*)

'At the time I took quite a bit of stick from certain quarters for signing Dennis, but Dennis was as good a signing as any I made.

'When you pay money (£175,000) for a player you don't look on it as a gamble and I never had any doubts about his ability. He was always a tremendous professional, not just within the team, but within the whole club. The standards at any club are set by the senior professionals. And he along with other senior professionals at that time were responsible for the standard Villa set and achieved. I appreciate the help he gave me and the example he set to the younger players at the club.'

** an excerpt from Dennis's testimonial brochure*

Gary Shaw (*Aston Villa team-mate*)
'Has Aston Villa ever spent a better £175,000 in the transfer market than on Dennis Mortimer? I doubt it. He was a well-respected captain in our dressing room and as a player, there wouldn't be many better that have ever worn the Villa shirt. We linked up together well as I liked to drop back into the hole and Dennis liked to get forward. I suppose the iconic goal that he scored at Villa Park against Liverpool in January 1981 would be our most famous link-up because of what that goal represented.'

Graeme Souness (*Liverpool and Scotland*)
'Dennis's name is permanently lodged in the front of my brain because I took a punch at him in the FA Youth Cup Final (in 1970) and was given my marching orders, deservedly so. Believe it or not, the only other time I was sent off in my career in England was for doing the same thing with Stan Ternent when I was playing for Boro against Carlisle. I'm honest enough to say, though, it was a different time then and you could get away with a lot more than today.

'Dennis was a year older than me, but I remember him always being a good athlete who could get around the park, he had a good technique and was competitive. He was an all-round good player and that's how I remember him throughout my career. He annoyed players because he nicked the ball off you and you couldn't catch him to leave something on him.

'When I was playing against Dennis, I knew I wouldn't have an easy game and had to be right up for it because of his technical ability, his mobility and his attitude. You're not captain of a club like Aston Villa if you have a stinking attitude; he was captain because the manager felt other players would want to follow his example, he set standards for the rest. He was unlucky not to play for England. With all due respect to Villa, if he had played for a more glamorous club like Liverpool or Manchester United or one of the bigger London clubs, he would have been an England player.

'That Villa team Dennis was part of, though, that won the league and European Cup was a very good team. Villa never gave us an easy ride and they spanked us a few times. You don't win a league unless you deserve it. At Liverpool we always put more importance on winning the league than the European Cup because it says more for your consistency over a long time, and Dennis's Villa team were very, very good.'

Kenny Swain (*Kirkby Boys district team and Aston Villa team-mate*)
'I played with Dennis for Kirkby Boys district team and

against him in school football also. By the time we were about 14, 15, you got to know who the best players were at the various schools and Dennis was the best at his school. He was a lightweight in those days, as we all were – probably undernourished! I remember him being a great athlete which remained the case throughout his career.

'He was a reliable, consistent player who always gave his all. There was no side to him other than being a good, honest, professional player.

'He made my move to Villa from Chelsea a lot more comfortable as we knew each other. When I met the manager Ron Saunders in his office on my first day, Dennis came in with me. It all just felt right, like hand in glove. Three Scousers sitting there! I felt at home, along with John Gidman who was also in the team then.

'I followed Dennis's career during the five or so years I was at Chelsea and was able to observe how he had developed quite a lot from his Coventry days. I thought, "Wow, what a good player Dennis has turned out to be." The same with Terry Mac.

'Dennis wasn't a cavalier captain but he was a model pro and everyone looked up to him. He was a figurehead and he reminded me of John Hollins, who I had the pleasure of playing with at Chelsea. There were all those cavalier characters at Stamford Bridge then but John stood out as the model pro.

'What I admired about Dennis, and still do, was his conviction in his methods. In fact, he earned a reputation as something of a hard taskmaster when he was a Football Association coach – he never gave a coach [taking his badges] an easy ride just because of who they were. He stuck to his beliefs and I admired him for that.

'I was mostly Dennis's room-mate through my time at Villa. He loved a cup of tea and was an interesting man who had passions outside of football like photography, reading and music. We used to argue about who loved their music more. My wife worked for The Beatles and met them lots of times so that gave me some bragging rights!'

Phil Thompson (*Kirkby Boys, Liverpool and England*) 'When you look at Dennis's career and the things that he won, I'm very pleased to hear that he's doing a book, more so his family will have that legacy as Dennis had a fabulous career.

'He lived a couple of hundred yards from me when we were kids in Kirkby. I remember his house by The Kingfisher pub and the 12/5 Club. We went to the same school, I knew his brothers, he was a friend of my older brother Owen, so we all knew one another and were brought up together. We had nothing else in our lives then other than football. That's all we knew, unlike the kids now.

'We both played for Kirkby Boys and it's extraordinary to think that such a small town has four European Cup winners in myself, Dennis, Kenny Swain and Terry McDermott.

'Even more extraordinary is that two lads from the same Kirkby school, me and Dennis, captained two different teams to European Cup glory within a year in 1981 and 1982.

'As opponents, Dennis played in the game I would rate as one of my all-time career disappointments when Villa beat Liverpool 5-1 [in 1976]. They probably had six shots and almost everything went in and it was 5-1 at half-time. That was against the best goalkeeper in the world in my opinion, Ray Clemence.

'That team Dennis was in then was a fantastic side. But I'd say the 1981 team was better, though, because the 5-1 was a one-off but to win a league means you've been the best team over a whole season. Then to win the European Cup as well, that's greatness. Their achievement was similar to Nottingham Forest as they were both dominant for one or two seasons. It's a shame they didn't sustain that success.

'After all those years playing against each other, it was nice for me and Dennis to share the same dressing room when we played together at Sheffield United at the end of our careers. It was quite incredible that two European Cup-winning captains came together on loan like that. That was a bloody tough league!'

Mark Walters (*Aston Villa team-mate*)
'Dennis Mortimer must be the best player there has ever been never to have played for England. He was an inspirational team-mate for me and was actually my room-mate on my first trip abroad which, I think, was

Bucharest. He was just a great pro who ate the right things, didn't drink, had a good physique and I imagine these are the reasons why the manager wanted me to room with him, to learn how to conduct myself and live in the right way off the field.

'This was the 1980s when it wasn't unusual for players to go out drinking on a Wednesday night and drive home. But that was not something Dennis would ever be involved with. As a character in the dressing room, he was also a respected figure. Dennis was a quiet guy most of the time, but he still had strong opinions and was never shy in coming forward to say anything that needed to be said. He was the perfect captain.

'One of the reasons I left Villa stemmed from the unhappiness I had at how the club treated Dennis. They dragged their feet in giving him a testimonial and let him go too early. I know I left a couple of seasons later, but I never forgot that. I always thought, "If Villa are happy enough to treat Dennis like that, how would they treat little Mark from Aston?" I told myself I would never stay for sentimental reasons after that, if ever my ambitions weren't met.'

Peter White (*former Midlands football reporter*)
'I first met Dennis in the early 1970s when he played for Coventry City, and I ghost-wrote his weekly column for the *Coventry Evening Telegraph*. He signed for Villa, and I later joined the *Sports Argus*, and again ghost-wrote his regular column, as well as many other stories with him.

'Dennis always had open, honest and forthright views, but I believe he did his best talking on the pitch, as a clever, tireless midfielder and magnificent leader, who set up and scored goals. For me, one of the best of his kind I've ever seen in a Villa shirt. He should have won many England caps, but somehow they eluded him.

'We were good friends away from football and spent many great social times together. Now we tend just to keep in touch by phone, with the occasional meet-up.

'I will always be indebted to Dennis for what he did for me in 1982. I went to Rotterdam as a "punter" on a coach from Villa Park, but with a press box ticket. After the game, Brendon Ormsby got me into the dressing room. Amid the celebrations I knew I had missed my coach home, but Dennis invited me to travel on the team coach to the team hotel in Amsterdam, allowed me into the after-match "private party", then let me fly home with the team to East Midlands airport the following day, where I was again given a place on the team coach for the trip back to Villa Park. I still have to pinch myself. It was all down to Dennis, with a little help from Brendon and Tony Barton – thanks, pal.'